Bridge Made Easy

Book Two
For Intermediates

by Caroline Sydnor

Published by
Devyn Press, Inc.
3600 Chamberlain Lane, Suite 230
Louisville, KY 40241
1-800-274-2221
Fax 502-426-2044

See the back cover for ordering information

First Printing September 1977
Second Printing April 1978
Third Printing March 1983
Fourth Printing October 1986
Fifth Printing March 1989
Sixth Printing April 1992
Seventh Printing April 2002
Eighth Printing March 2005

ISBN 0-939460-80-7

Dedicated to Al and Walter

"I know of no greater pleasure than to do a good deed by stealth, and be discovered by accident." Alec Woollcott

Former President Gerald Ford accepts a copy of **Bridge Made Easy** from the author. Betty Ford says her husband is "the bridge player in the family."

FOREWORD

The most popular game in the world — indoor or outdoor — is contract bridge. There are 40,000,000 players in the United States alone. Almost anyone can learn to play and play well—young and old, strong and weak, rich and poor.

The better you play, the more fun you'll have, and the more people will want you for a partner. This book is to help the casual player learn to bid better and play better.

The first giant step is the technique of handling 20 specific card plays that occur over and over again. One of them crops up in almost every hand and the good player knows instantly how to handle each one. A student who had played bridge 20 years said he had never *heard* of the double finesse. "That lesson alone was worth my $25 class fee," James Whitsett declared. After mastering these card plays, Jim began talking about how "lucky" he was getting at bridge.

Also full of "luck" are the other nine giant steps in this book — learning when to hold back a Big Card (ducking), how to send messages to your partner with your small cards (signaling), the art of defensive bidding, the science behind the rebid by the opener, and so forth.

In the tests you confront immediately the points of the lesson, helping you learn faster. Taking one is probably equivalent in experience to a week of actual play. If you miss more than three questions, re-read the chapter and try again.

The four hands that follow concentrate on the same features, so you meet the lesson a third time, now with cards in your hand. If you misplay, do not be discouraged. Experts make mistakes. One of the challenges of bridge is that you can always improve.

Remember, too, bridge is a game. Have fun!

THANK YOU!

Friends, fellow bridge teachers, and students — more than I can list — helped me with this book and I am grateful.

Especially, I thank Marion Galland, the "pickiest" proof reader I know, who read copy for me and made many useful suggestions for this book and for the first volume.

Lenore Macen, my student and friend, patiently typed, many times on precious weekends. ("Is this the last chapter, Caroline?" . . . "No" . . . "Oh.")

Jim Coldsmith, editor of the *Port Packet,* where some of the hands originally appeared in my column, graciously consented to my using them again.

Becky Levering, who has taught bridge in Baltimore for 20 years, guiding more than 5,000 students, tested the preliminary manuscript in her classes. She prepared a careful critique, and contributed three hands.

Carole Amster also tested this course in her classes in Fairfax, Va., and offered me sound advice. She designed the hand on lead-directing doubles.

David Flaumenhaft, of North Woodmere, N.Y., examined the original draft, made recommendations, and supplied a hand. David draws classes as large as 60 from the New York City area.

CONTENTS

CARD PLAYS IN HANDS

I. CARD PLAYS THAT CREATE TRICKS

"He's lucky at cards," you hear people say. "He wins all the time." To be lucky at cards is an art which you can master. Everyone is dealt the same number of Aces and Kings and Queens. Some people just play theirs better. If you want to win more, learn to finesse. It's the greatest way to create tricks in bridge.

It's easy to win tricks when you hold all top cards in a solid sequence — ♠AKQJ ♡AKQ ♢AKQ ♣AKQ. But it takes a card player to pull in a trick with a card that isn't high. Remove an honor (or two) from the middle of those sequences — ♠AQJ9 ♡AJ10 ♢AQ10 ♣AJ9 — and you need technique.

If you hold the Ace and King of Spades, you expect to win two tricks. Holding the Ace and Queen you also can take two tricks if you play with skill and if the King is in the right spot.

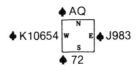

You have one trick; you want two. Lead *toward* your big card, lead low from the South hand. If the second hand plays a low card, you risk the card that isn't high, the Queen. If the King is in the second hand, you can trap it. Here's the secret: You forced the person with a crucial card to play before you put up a big card. It's called a finesse.

If you familiarize yourself with finesses, it will give you a tremendous advantage at the bridge table. Almost every hand you play as declarer has one. It will help to take the 13 cards of one suit and actually lay out each of these card combinations and play them.

The Single Finesse

The single finesse is the simplest. You are missing a big face card but you don't want to lose a trick to it. Half the time the missing honor will be dealt to your right-hand opponent and half the time to your left-hand opponent. It's a 50-50 proposition. If you always finesse, you'll win half the time.

They dealt you two tricks but you want three. Lead the Queen, if West plays low, you play low; if West covers, you cover. If West, the second player, has the King, you'll trap it.

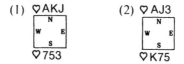

(1) You were dealt two tricks, the Ace and King, but you want three. Lead a low card from the South hand and put in the Jack. With plenty of entries, play the King first, to guard against a singleton Queen, and then (using another suit) go back to the South hand to lead toward the Ace-Jack and finesse the Jack.

(2) Here you have the same cards in a different holding. First play the King (the single honor) and then lead toward the double honor and finesse the Jack.

The Double Finesse

The double finesse is just what the name implies; you are missing two crucial cards and you want to trap one or both of them. You want to master this because it's one of the best percentage plays in bridge. The two outstanding honors will usually be divided between your opponents. Consequently, you can create an extra trick 75% of the time!

$\Diamond$ AQ10

N
W   E
S

$\Diamond$ 952

You were dealt one trick, the Ace, but you're longing to get two. Lead from the South hand, toward the big cards, and risk the 10. If it loses to the Jack, go back to the South hand (in another suit), lead low, and try the Queen. Without seeing the opponents' cards, an experienced card player knows four possible situations could exist. West could have (1) the King, (2) the Jack, (3) the King and the Jack, or (4) neither. In three of the four cases, you win an extra trick, and in the fourth you fail. That's a 75% chance to bring in an extra trick.

Most of the time this card play is going to bring you a bonus, but when Lady Luck blows her favors the other way — as she will 25% of the time — don't be discouraged. Shrug your shoulders; reassure yourself that the next three times she'll smile on you — if you play your cards correctly.

Here's another way you might hold the same cards:

◊ A52

◊ Q109

It's just another double finesse. Lead the 10 from your hand and cover if the next player covers and don't if he doesn't. If you lose to the Jack, return to your hand (in another suit) and lead the Queen. If your left hand opponent covers, you cover. The King will usually be in one opponent's hand and the Jack in the other, so 75% of the time, you'll bring in two tricks. The 9 is necessary for this play. (The 10 is a slightly better lead than the Queen because it succeeds in bringing in the whole suit on the rare occasion when you find the singleton King on your left; you can now finesse for the Jack on your right.)

♡ AJ10

♡ 765

Two honors are missing and you hope West has one of them. To win two tricks, lead a low card from South and put in the 10. If it loses to the Queen (or King), go back to South (in another suit), lead low, and, if West plays small, insert the Jack. It's another 75% play.

Did you know the AJ9 is just as good as the AJ10 *if* the 10 happens to be on your lucky side?

♡ AJ9

♡ K104   ♡ Q832

♡ 765

Lead small from the South hand, if West plays low, finesse the 9. (If West plays the 10, you play the Jack.) If East wins with a high honor, next time lead from South and finesse the Jack.

You must lose to the Ace no matter who has it, but you can avoid losing to the Queen if West has it. To win two tricks, lead low from the South hand and put in the 10. If the Ace wins, go back to your hand (in another suit) and finesse the Jack.

Tip:

When you can lead a card that will keep you in the proper hand ready for a second finesse, do so:

Lead the Jack and if the finesse wins, you're still in the strategic hand, ready to make the same play again.

Leading Toward an Honor

This combination will yield a trick whenever the Ace is held by West. Lead a little card from the South hand, playing *toward* your honor. If West plays the Ace, you play low and the King has become a winner. Many times a good player in West's chair will play low even with the Ace, hoping you'll lose your nerve. Be brave. If he plays low, you reach over, pick up that King and play it. It's now or never. You know they won't let you win it the next time around when it's a singleton. This play will win half the time and lose half the time. If you're afraid to play the King, you'll never win a trick with it. Bridge is not a game for the weak of heart!

You have a trick, the Ace of Spades, but you want two. Play the Ace and then lead low *toward* the Queen. If West plays low, you put in the Queen. Notice that this is not a finessing situation because you don't have any supporting honors for the Queen.

Again you have one trick but you need two. Lead a low card *toward* the Queen. Do not play the Ace first. You'll make two tricks anytime West has the King.

You have two tricks but you'd like to win three. Lead low from your hand toward the Jack. If West has the Queen, you're in clover. If he plays the Queen, you play low. If West plays a low card, pull out the Jack.

♠ QJ54

♠ A732

What is your best play to lose only one trick? Play the Ace and lead low to the Jack. If this wins, return to your hand and lead low toward the Queen. This is not a finessing play because you don't hold the 10. When the outstanding cards are divided 3-2, you'll always lose one trick and one trick only. This play protects you when the outstanding cards are 4-1 with the four in the West hand.

♠ Q975

♠ K642

If the bidding has indicated one opponent — say East — is more likely to have the Ace, play a low card from dummy through East toward your King. This guards against a singleton Ace capturing an honor. If East plays low and the King wins, continue with a low card and duck all around, hoping the Ace is now bare. (There is no logic to going up with the Queen because it is certain to be topped by the Ace.) If East started with ♠ Ax, his Ace will fall "on air" and you will win three tricks.

♠ K983

♠ AQ1072

This is your trump suit and you cannot afford to lose a trick. The only threat is one opponent might have all four missing cards. Play a high card first from the hand with two top honors in it, thus saving a high honor in each hand for a later finesse if needed. Play the Ace first, and if East shows out, next lead from your hand and finesse the 9.

Cover an Honor with an Honor

What are the defenders doing all the while declarer is making his finesses? When the declarer leads a small card toward a tenace*, the defense is powerless. All a defender can do is play smoothly, pretend to have no interest in the suit, and pray declarer will lose his nerve. The missing honor is either right or wrong, and the defenders cannot change where it is.

Sometimes declarer leads an honor and the defender with a higher honor has a choice of covering or not covering. He can play the King on the Queen or the Queen on the Jack forcing declarer to play a still higher honor on the same trick. This takes *two* of declarer's honors to win *one* trick. With high cards out of the way, juniors are promoted into winners. This is good for the defenders when they hold the juniors.

There is an adage, "Cover an honor with an honor *whenever you can promote a card in your hand or in partner's.*" Here's an example:

◊ AQ1054

◊ K7 | W   E | ◊ 9862

◊ J3

South leads the Jack hoping to find West with the King. If the outstanding cards are evenly divided, it's possible to

---

**A tenace is two honors in the same suit not in sequence, AQ or KJ.*

win five tricks. Suppose the King is right but the suit breaks 4-2? That is where West has a chance to be a hero. The correct play is to cover the Jack with the King, forcing declarer to play the Ace to win the trick. The second round will be won by the Queen and the third by the 10. What about the fourth round? By covering an honor with an honor, West promoted partner's 9 into a winner.

West went up with the King only because declarer led an honor. If declarer had led a small card, West would have played a small card.

When Not to Cover

You can decide when to cover an honor with an honor by using common sense. There are exceptions to the rule which you can work out by taking a little time to think it through.

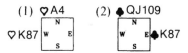

(1) If South leads the Queen of trumps, West should not cover because he can see he's longer in the suit than dummy and his King cannot be caught. The Ace will have to be played on the second round and the King will become the master card.

(2) The Queen is led from dummy. Should East cover? No, he cannot set up a card for his partner or himself.

(3) ◊ QJ92

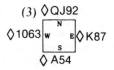

◊ 1063　◊ K87

◊ A54

(3) Declarer leads the Queen from dummy. Should East cover? No. He should wait to cover the second honor, the Jack. Why? If he covers the Queen, declarer can now take a finesse against partner's 10.

I. Test Your Card Play

You are South playing these combinations of cards with plenty of entries to either hand. Circle the cards you would play to win the most tricks. Assuming the second player lays down a little card, draw an arrow to the card you would play from the third hand.

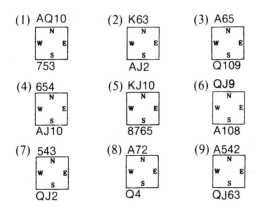

(1) AQ10
753

(2) K63
AJ2

(3) A65
Q109

(4) 654
AJ10

(5) KJ10
8765

(6) QJ9
A108

(7) 543
QJ2

(8) A72
Q4

(9) A542
QJ63

Declarer leads the Queen from dummy. What should East play?

(10) QJ10 — E K742

(11) QJ6 — E K54

(12) Q73 — E K5

South leads the 2 from his hand. What does West play?

(13) AQ10
K73 — S 2

1. Creating Winners

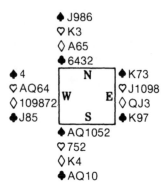

```
              ♠ J986
              ♡ K3
              ◊ A65
              ♣ 6432
   ♠ 4          ┌─────────┐    ♠ K73
   ♡ AQ64       │    N    │    ♡ J1098
   ◊ 109872   W │         │ E  ◊ QJ3
   ♣ J85        │    S    │    ♣ K97
              └─────────┘
              ♠ AQ1052
              ♡ 752
              ◊ K4
              ♣ AQ10
```

South deals
North-South vulnerable
The bidding:

South	West	North	East
1 Spade	Pass	2 Spades	Pass
3 Spades	Pass	4 Spades	All pass

There is a deck of cards that will deal quickly this identical hand, and all the other hands in *Bridge Made Easy, Volume II.*

For the deck to work, the deal must rotate as it does in regular bridge. South deals hand 1, automatically receiving the cards printed in the South hand above. West deals hand 2, North hand 3, and East hand 4. Thus it follows throughout.

(To order cards see back cover.)

HOW TO DEAL

the 40 hands in

Bridge Made Easy

Vol. II

For Intermediates

For hand 1, deal the card to the person in the same position at the table as the dot is to the number:

when the dot is at the top of the number deal the card to the player opposite you.

when the dot is on the right, deal the card to the player on your right.

when the dot is under the number deal the card to yourself.

when the dot is on the left, deal the card to the player on your left.

The deal rotates as in regular bridge.

Caroline's Cards

211 So. Lee Street

Alexandria, Va. 22314

*Certain card plays arise over and over again — the single finesse, the double finesse, and leading **toward** an honor. There is one in almost every hand you play. They are the meat-and-potato plays and a declarer who can manage them is going to be a winner.*

The souffle plays — the single squeeze, the double squeeze, the trump coup, the Deschapelles coup — seldom come up and aren't nearly as important.

When North gave a single raise, South, with 17 values, invited game by bidding 3 Spades. North, on the top of his raise, went to game.

West led the Diamond 10 and declarer went up with dummy's Ace to be ready for the trump finesse. He rolled out the Spade Jack, East played low and so did everyone else. (From the bidding, East reasoned his partner had only one trump. Don't cover a trump honor when you hold three cards in the suit, unless you can set up a card for yourself.) Now declarer pulled out the Spade 9 and it won, too.

Realizing the need to lead Clubs twice from dummy for the double finesse and woefully short of entries, he switched to the Club deuce, inserted the 10, and West happily grabbed the Jack. Another Diamond was captured by declarer's King, and the trump Ace collected the King, the last outstanding trump.

Declarer led a low Heart. West decided it was time to take the Ace and try Diamonds again. But declarer walked out with a trump. Entering dummy with the Heart King, declarer repeated the Club finesse and the Queen held. His work was done; all the others were winners. He turned 11 tricks.

South held five potential losers and could have gone down. Good card play technique and a little luck whittled those losers down to two, nailing down his game plus an overtrick.

2. Leading *Toward* Is Winner's Way

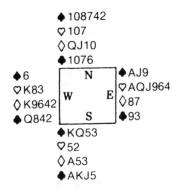

```
                    ♠ 108742
                    ♡ 107
                    ◇ QJ10
                    ♣ 1076
         ♠ 6            N          ♠ AJ9
         ♡ K83                     ♡ AQJ964
         ◇ K9642    W      E       ◇ 87
         ♣ Q842        S           ♣ 93
                    ♠ KQ53
                    ♡ 52
                    ◇ A53
                    ♣ AKJ5
```

West deals

The bidding:

West	North	East	South
Pass	Pass	1 Heart	Double
3 Hearts	Pass	4 Hearts	Double
All Pass			

When the auction reverted to West he jumped the bidding to show values just under an opening hand. Having previously passed he couldn't force partner to bid again — nor could he hold 10 high-card points or he would have redoubled.

East was delighted to carry on to game and South, looking at five potential winners, cracked it.

South led the Club King, winning trick one, and shifted to a trump to protect his Spade honors from dummy's ruffing power. East won in the closed hand and returned the Diamond 7, leading *toward* the King. South played the Ace and laid down another trump. Lo, all the outstanding Hearts came tumbling down as declarer won in his own hand.

Declarer led a Diamond to dummy's King and continued another Diamond, ruffing in his hand. Everyone followed so dummy's Diamonds were established!

East cashed the Spade Ace, ruffed a Spade in dummy, then played dummy's good Diamonds, discarding a Club and a Spade in the closed hand.

Thus declarer landed his contract and an overtrick.

3. Playing Percentages

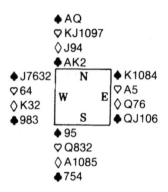

```
              ♠ AQ
              ♡ KJ1097
              ◊ J94
              ♣ AK2
♠ J7632    ┌─────────┐   ♠ K1084
♡ 64       │    N    │   ♡ A5
◊ K32      │ W     E │   ◊ Q76
♣ 983      │    S    │   ♣ QJ106
           └─────────┘
              ♠ 95
              ♡ Q832
              ◊ A1085
              ♣ 754
```

North deals

The bidding:

North	East	South	West
1 Heart	Double	2 Hearts	Pass
4 Hearts	All pass		

"You're lucky at cards," complained East when North chalked up his game. "You win all the time." North didn't answer. Here's the play that aroused East's ire.

The opening lead was the Club Queen and declarer won the King. In a fast study of his resources, North counted four Heart winners, one Spade, one Diamond, and two Clubs, bringing the total to eight. Looking for more, he spotted the Spade suit with the King missing, and the Diamond suit with the King and Queen missing.

Starting after trumps, North led the Heart 10 and won it. Next, he played the Heart 9 and East collected his Ace as all the outstanding trumps fell. East pursued Clubs with the

Jack and declarer climbed up with the Ace. He laid down the Diamond Jack, which succumbed to West's King.

West returned the Club 9, which won as East carefully stayed under it with the 6. East-West were book-in. Now West switched to the Spade 3. (East began to drool at the prospect of the setting trick.)

Spurning the finesse, North went up with the Ace. Acting like a man of authority, he led the Diamond 9. East followed low and so did dummy. It captured the trick. Declarer continued a baby Diamond, the Queen fell, and North covered her with dummy's Ace. Joyfully, he cashed dummy's Diamond 10, discarding his Spade Queen. He squeaked through with his contract.

Mr. Lucky's double finesse in Diamonds is one of the best percentage plays in bridge. He had a 75% chance to win three tricks. The Spade finesse was only a 50% play, and he wouldn't need it at all if the Diamonds behaved.

He hung his hat on the 75% play.

Lucky?

4. When *Not* To Finesse

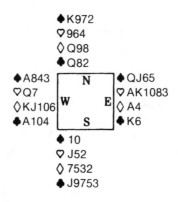

```
              ♠K972
              ♡964
              ◊Q98
              ♣Q82
 ♠A843      ┌─────────┐    ♠QJ65
 ♡Q7        │    N    │    ♡AK1083
 ◊KJ106     │ W     E │    ◊A4
 ♣A104      │    S    │    ♣K6
            └─────────┘
              ♠ 10
              ♡J52
              ◊7532
              ♣J9753
```

East deals
The bidding:

East	South	West	North
1 Heart	Pass	1 Spade	Pass
4 Spades	Pass	4 NT	Pass
5 Hearts	Pass	6 Spades	All Pass

In the Open Pair event at a 1976 tournament in Washington, D.C., players met this hand. At 24 tables checked, 18 West players brought in their little slam. The other six went astray.

At my table, my partner led the Diamond 8 and declarer took advantage of it by letting it ride to his 10. West held no losers in the side suits. His only problem was handling trumps. He went to dummy with the Diamond Ace to lead the Spade Queen and finesse. North won the King and now declarer was dead. He had to lose one more trump.

West was mesmerized by the prospect of a Spade finesse, but he didn't have a finessing situation because he didn't have the 10. His job was to play that suit the safest way he could to lose only one trick. If the outstanding Spades are divided 3-2, he's safe. He can play it anyway. What if they are split 4-1? Correct play is to lay down the Ace (in case there's a singleton King floating around the table), and lead low toward dummy's honors. If North plays low, go up with the Jack. Then come back to the West hand in another suit, and lead low toward dummy's Queen.

One of the first lessons the bridge student learns is how to finesse. It is the most important play in bridge, cropping up again and again. More difficult to master is when *not* to finesse.

II. NO TRUMP
Two New Friends, Stayman and Gerber

You bid to describe the 13 cards you hold to your partner, to tell him how many face cards you have and how your cards are distributed among the suits. Sometimes it takes several bids to do this and the more bids it takes, the greater the chance for an error. An opening No Trump telegraphs all this valuable information in one call. Consequently, an auction that begins with a No Trump seldom goes wrong. With such a clear picture of partner's hand, the responder can envision how the 26 cards mesh, and gauge the best final contract with high accuracy. The opening No Trump formula is:

1 No Trump, 16-18 points and three suits protected
2 No Trump, 22-24 points and all suits protected
3 No Trump, 25-27 points and all suits protected

Each is limited to a specific three points, no more, no less. Distribution is even, 4-3-3-3, 4-4-3-2, or 5-3-3-2. There can be no void, no singleton, and only one doubleton.

Having so vividly described his hand, the No Trump opener doesn't bid again, unless partner asks him a question. The responder has become the captain and guides the auction to the best spot. It's one of the few times in bridge when the weak hand is in command. The responder bases his decisions on:

26 points will usually produce game
33 points a little slam
37 points a grand slam

The responder simply adds his values to the precise number opener advertised and bids this way:

Responding to 1 NT with Even Distribution

With 0-7, pass. No game is in sight

With 8-9, bid 2 NT, inviting partner to bid game with 17 or 18

With 10-14, bid 3 NT

With 15-16, bid 4 NT, inviting partner to bid 6 NT with 17 or 18

With 17-18, bid 6 NT

With 19-20, bid 5 NT, a command for partner to bid 6 NT with a minimum and 7 NT with 17 or 18

With 21, bid 7 NT

Distribution in the responder's hand is a vital clue in choosing a contract. When the responder has uneven distribution and a long major, it is wiser to play in that major. It takes the same 26 points to bring in 4 Spades or 4 Hearts. It's much safer because the opponents can't run a long suit; you can stop them with a ruff.

With values for a game and a six-card major, the responder knows the partnership has a trump suit. By inference, the opener has at least a doubleton. He jumps to game in his suit. With a five-card major he jumps only to 3 Spades or 3 Hearts. Opener, with only a doubleton, returns to No Trump, but with trump support bids game in the major.

When the responder has a long suit and a poor hand, he bids only two of his suit — 2 Spades, 2 Hearts, or 2 Diamonds. These are "stop" bids. Since he didn't jump he wants to close the auction. (A rescue of 2 Clubs is unavailable; it's reserved for the valuable Stayman Convention which we learn next.) To summarize:

Responding to 1 NT with Uneven Distribution

With 0-7 and a five-card or six-card suit, rescue with
  2♣, 2♥, or 2♦. Example, with ♠J10xxxx ♥x
  ♦xxxx ♣xx, bid 2♠, a sign-off
With 8 or 9 and a five-card major, bid 2♣ (Stayman)
With 10 and a five-card major, jump to 3♠ or 3♥
With 10 and a six-card major, jump to 4♠ or 4♥
Conceal a long minor. With 8 or 9, bid 2 NT, with 10 bid
  3 NT

Here's Stayman

It is also possible for the partnership to have an eight-card trump suit with the cards divided four in one hand and four in the other:

♠QJ98

♠AK107

This holding will bring in only four tricks in a No Trump, but played in a Spade contract, with dummy holding a short suit, the ruffing power will bring in extra tricks.

There is a way to unveil this 4-4 fit in a major. It's called the Stayman Convention after Sam Stayman, the New York expert, who developed this safety device to help on that special hand. It is the most important convention in bridge after Blackwood.

Here's the procedure. When partner opens 1 No Trump and the responder holds:

  •At least one four-card major
  •8 high-card points or more
  •One or more points in distribution

the responder bids 2 Clubs. This is an artificial bid; it has nothing to do with the Club suit. It asks partner, "Did you open the bidding with a four-card major?" It is a forcing bid; partner must answer. The answers are:

> "2 Spades" with four or more Spades
> "2 Hearts" with four or more Hearts
> "2 Diamonds" with neither

Let's practice it. Your partner opened 1 No Trump. What would you respond holding:

1. ♠ K963 ♡ AK52 ◊ Q952 ♣ 9
2. ♠ K852 ♡ AJ642 ◊ 64 ♣ 72
3. ♠ KJ43 ♡ Q72 ◊ Q94 ♣ J53
4. ♠ 72 ♡ AKJ972 ◊ Q72 ♣ 85
5. ♠ J763 ♡ K842 ◊ J63 ♣ 92

(1) Bid 2 Clubs, Stayman. With 12 high-card points you're going to go to game but you hope it can be in Hearts or Spades.

(2) It's 2 Clubs. If partner bids 2 Diamonds denying four cards in either major, you will now bid 2 Hearts showing your five-card suit and a minimum hand. (You had to have 8 points to employ Stayman.) With 10 points or more, you would *jump* to 3 Hearts.

(3) Say 2 No Trump. You have no distributional point. Don't increase the contract when you can't trump anything.

(4) Bid 4 Hearts. You already know you have a trump suit.

(5) Pass. You have both majors but not the eight points needed to initiate Stayman.

Answering the Stayman Question

Now let's move to the other side of the table — be the No Trump opener — and respond to Stayman.

1NT | 2♣

?

1. ♠A765 ♡KQ4 ◊AJ3 ♣Q85
2. ♠KJ4 ♡K764 ◊AQ2 ♣A73
3. ♠Q72 ♡AJ7 ◊K2 ♣AQJ42

(1) Bid 2 Spades, (2) it's 2 Hearts, and (3) it's 2 Diamonds, an artificial bid, which has nothing to do with the Diamond suit.

What Next?

Now the ball bounces back to the Stayman bidder who announces whether a trump suit has been found and gives his point count:

• With four cards in the same major and 8 or 9 points, invite game with a single raise to 3 Hearts or 3 Spades.

• With four cards in the same major and 10 to 14 points, jump to 4 Hearts or 4 Spades.

• Without a trump fit and 8 or 9 points bid 2 No Trump, with 10-14 jump to 3 No Trump.

Rebid by the Opener

If the responder bid game, the opener passes. On borderline hands when the responder invites game by increasing the contract but stops short of game with a bid of 2 No Trump, 3 Hearts, or 3 Spades, opener passes with 16 and bids game with 17 or 18.

In answering Stayman, the opener sometimes finds himself with an embarrassment of riches because he holds four cards in both majors. He can bid either first. With the popularity of up-the-line bidding many players answer Hearts first. It doesn't matter which. If partner denies interest in that major by bidding 2 No Trump, the *opener* should correct to 3 of the other major with a minimum hand and 4 with a maximum. When partner went into the Stayman convention, he promised four of a major; if he doesn't have Hearts, he must have Spades. Over responder's rebid of 3 No Trump, correct to 4 of the other major.

Let's experiment on a possible auction:

You	Partner
1 NT	2 Clubs
2 Hearts	2 No Trump
?	

1.♠AK72 ♡KQ32 ♢Q65 ♣Q2
2.♠KQ43 ♡AQJ3 ♢Q42 ♣K3

(1) Bid 3 Spades. Partner employed Stayman; if he doesn't have four cards in the Heart suit he has four in the Spade suit. You say only 3 because you're minimum. (2) It's 4 Spades. With a maximum go to game.

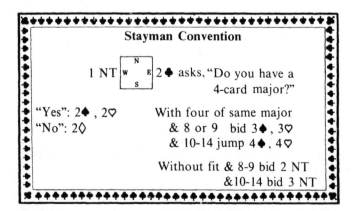

Stayman Convention

1 NT [N W E S] 2♣ asks, "Do you have a 4-card major?"

"Yes": 2♠, 2♡   With four of same major
"No": 2♢   & 8 or 9 bid 3♠, 3♡
                     & 10-14 jump 4♠, 4♡

Without fit & 8-9 bid 2 NT
            &10-14 bid 3 NT

Responding to 2 NT or 3 NT

When your partner opens 2 No Trump, any response is a move toward game. With 0-3 points, pass. Be realistic and don't expect partner to have more than 22 points. Even if he has the 24-point maximum he needs entries to dummy to make his card plays.

With even distribution and 4 points, bid 3 No Trump; with 9 or 10 jump to 4 No Trump to invite a slam; with 11 you can bid 6 No Trump.

Holding a long major, bid your suit. With six cards jump to game. With five cards bid 3 of your major and let partner choose between No Trump and the major. Employ Stayman by bidding 3 Clubs.

An opening 3 No Trump is rare, but if your partner bids it, add your points to his, use your common sense, and proceed accordingly. The Stayman bid is not available.

How To Open Other Balanced Hands

When you have a balanced hand and too few points to open 1 No Trump — or too many — it takes two bids to tell your story:

With 13-15, open one in a suit and rebid No Trump at the lowest level. You - 1♡, Partner - 1♠, You - 1 NT.

With 19, open one of a suit. At your next bid, with stoppers in all unbid suits, *jump* the bidding one level in No Trump. You - 1 ♡, Partner - 1 ♠, You - 2 NT. Or, You - 1 ♡, Partner - 2 ◊, You - 3 NT.

With 20 or 21, open one in a suit. Then, *double jump* to 3 No Trump. You - 1♡, Partner - 1♠, You - 3 NT.

Gerber Convention

Sometimes the responder has a good hand with a long, strong suit that will bring in lots of tricks, but he doesn't have the points necessary to bid a slam. Suppose your partner opened 1 No Trump and you held ♠KQJ ♡xx ◊ KQ10xxxx ♣ x. You'd like to be in a slam if partner held enough Aces. How can you find out how many he has? The Blackwood bid is only available in suit contracts, because in a No Trump auction a bid of 4 No Trump is quantitative, showing a specific number of points.

There is a special way to ask for Aces when your partner opens in No Trump—the Gerber convention, designed by John Gerber of Houston, Texas. It is to jump to 4 Clubs, an artificial bid, which asks, "How many Aces do you have?" The responses are:

with no Aces bid 4 ◊
with one Ace bid 4 ♡
with two Aces bid 4 ♠
with three Aces bid 4 NT
with four aces bid 4 ◊

There is no problem understanding whether the 4 Diamond bid shows all the Aces or none. Four Aces are a lot of points and all that count would show in the bidding. Provided the partnership holds all the Aces, the Gerber bidder may ask for Kings by bidding 5 Clubs. The responses are similar:

with no Kings bid 5 ◊
with one King bid 5 ♡
with two Kings bid 5 ♠
with three Kings bid 5 NT
with four Kings bid 5 ◊

II. Test Your No Trump, Stayman, and Gerber

Your partner opened 1 No Trump. What's your response holding:

1. ♠AQ83 ♡Q7 ◊K107632 ♣2
2. ♣842 ♡AQ84 ◊Q965 ♣54
3. ♠AQ74 ♡A74 ◊875 ♣864
4. ♣1098765 ♡Q4 ◊864 ♣64
5. ♣85 ♡KQ1073 ◊J43 ♣A72
6. ♠AJ8 ♡AQ ◊K764 ♣K764
7. ♠AJ874 ♡K932 ◊85 ♣32
8. ♠986 ♡1094 ◊75 ♣KJ987

You opened 1 No Trump, your partner responded 2 Clubs, what's your rebid?

9. ♠9752 ♡AQ7 ◊AJ4 ♣KQJ
10. ♣QJ5 ♡AK5 ◊Q4 ♣AJ864

Partner opened 1 No Trump and the next player overcalled 2 Spades. What would you bid holding these:

11. ♠Q1094 ♡4 ◊AK72 ♣J982
12. ♣9 ♡Q1096 ◊AQ72 ♣K862

Partner opened 2 No Trump. What's your bid on:

13. ♠5 ♡1094 ◊KQ98765 ♣K4
14. ♠A863 ♡Q654 ◊8765 ♣7

5. Stayman Steers You Right

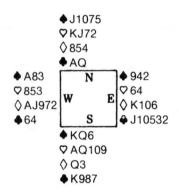

North deals

The bidding:

North	East	South	West
Pass	Pass	1 NT	Pass
2 Clubs	Pass	2 Hearts	Pass
4 Hearts	All Pass		

West led the Club 6, the top of a doubleton. Declarer went up with dummy's Ace as East followed with the Club 2.

Declarer ran three rounds of trumps to bring in all the opponent's Hearts. On the third round, East discarded the Spade 2. Next, declarer played the King of Spades and West won the Ace.

It was West's moment in the spotlight. His partner had said, "I don't like Clubs" when he laid down the 2 at trick one. Then he said, "I don't have anything in Spades" when he played that 2. West surmised his partner must have something in Diamonds so he pulled out the Diamond Ace and saw his partner contribute the 10, an obvious come-on signal. West continued with a low Diamond and East won the King, dropping declarer's Queen. East continued Diamonds but declarer trumped and took all the rest.

Without the Stayman Convention South and North would have sailed into a 3 No Trump contract, West would have opened his long Diamond suit, and East-West would have taken the first five tricks. Stayman steered them to the right contract and helped them find their 4-4 fit in a major suit.

6. Licking Lurking Losers

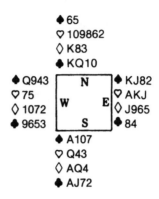

East deals

The bidding:

East	South	West	North
1 Diamond	1 NT	Pass	2 Clubs
Pass	2 Diamonds	Pass	2 Hearts
Pass	4 Hearts	All pass	

After East opened a Diamond, South overcalled a No Trump, and North began Stayman with a bid of 2 Clubs, asking his partner if he held a four-card major. South answered in the negative by bidding 2 Diamonds. Now, North called 2 Hearts showing precisely a hand with a five card suit and 8 or 9 points. South, with trump support and 17 highs, contracted for a game.

East led a baby Diamond. Declarer took a moment to analyze his cards, and found four losers lurking there — a Spade, the Ace and King of trumps, and possibly the Jack of trumps. He began to maneuver to avoid losing to the Jack. He let the Diamond ride to his King to get to his hand.

Placing East with the outstanding high cards, he wanted to lead Hearts *toward* dummy's Queen, making East play before dummy.

Tackling Hearts, he played the 10. East won the King and returned a Diamond to stick North on the board (hoping he'd err and pull a trump from dummy). Dummy's Diamond Queen won, but the declarer moved over to Clubs, playing a little one to his King to land back in his hand. He repeated the trump play *toward* dummy. East climbed up with the Ace.

Desperate, East switched to his last Club, hoping partner held the Queen, and could return the suit to let him win the Heart Jack. Alas, declarer held that lady too and won the trick. He rolled out another Heart and the Jack crumbled under dummy's Queen. His work was done. It was easy now to turn the rest of his 10 tricks.

Good defense would set a 3 No Trump contract. No strategy could set North's gilt-edged contract the way he played the hand.

7. Just a Little Squeeze

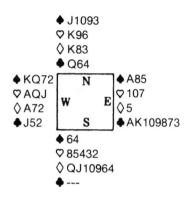

♠ J1093
♡ K96
◇ K83
♣ Q64

♠ KQ72   ♠ A85
♡ AQJ   ♡ 107
◇ A72   ◇ 5
♣ J52   ♣ AK109873

♠ 64
♡ 85432
◇ QJ10964
♣ ---

South deals

The bidding:

South	West	North	East
Pass	1 NT	Pass	4 Clubs
Pass	4 Spades	Pass	6 Clubs

After West opened a No Trump, East started thinking big. He had only 11 high-card points but he estimated his hand would bring in eight tricks. Slam-minded, he used Gerber to check for Aces, found all bases covered, and bid 6 Clubs. South started with the Diamond Queen.

East carefully counted his tricks — seven Clubs, three Spades, and two red Aces — then brought out the Diamond Ace. He led a baby Club to the King. Unable to follow, South carefully contributed a Spade. (He hoped declarer would notice the color, but miss the suit.)

East was wide-awake. He returned to the board with the Spade King and played the Club Jack. Nonchalantly, North played low, but so did declarer, the Jack winning.

Now East rattled off all his Clubs. (He had his contract but he wanted to outfox the opponents for an overtrick.) In the dummy he discarded two little Diamonds and the Heart Jack, while North threw the Heart 9 and two Diamonds, leaving this situation:

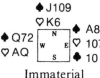

♠ J109
♡ K6

♠ Q72   ♠ A8
♡ AQ   ♡ 107
               ♣ 10

Immaterial

East led the Club 10 and pitched the Heart Queen from dummy. North was squeezed! He had to protect Spades and Hearts and he didn't have a card to spare. Finally, he threw the Heart 6. Declarer led to the Heart Ace and the King fell under it. He took the Spade Queen, then went to his hand with the Spade Ace. Declarer held out his last card, the Heart 10. It was top dog!

Whenever you have a long suit and you want an extra trick, run the suit. If one opponent has to protect two suits, he's helpless. It's called a squeeze.

8. Prudent Player Plans

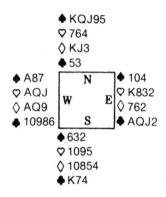

♠ KQJ95
♡ 764
◇ KJ3
♣ 53

♠ A87   ♠ 104
♡ AQJ   ♡ K832
◇ AQ9   ◇ 762
♣ 10986   ♣ AQJ2

N
W E
S

♠ 632
♡ 1095
◇ 10854
♣ K74

West deals

The bidding:

West	North	East	South
1 NT	Pass	2 Clubs	Pass
2 Diamonds	Pass	3 NT	All Pass

When West opened a No Trump, East made a Stayman try, but it failed. Then East contracted for the No Trump game. Eagerly, North led the Spade King. He saw he had a chance to sink this contract.

Declarer stopped a second to study strategy. He was positive of seven tricks, four Hearts and an Ace in each of the other suits. He could win two or three extra Clubs, depending on the location of the King. If North held that crucial card, he could finesse it, making 4 No Trump. If South held it, he'd lose to the King, and South would make the damaging Spade return. He couldn't stand that. West, a prudent player, decided to hold back his Spade Ace as long as he could, hoping to eliminate Spades from the South hand.

North won the King and continued the Queen, which won also. North led a third round, and declarer took the Ace. He laid down the Club 10 which lost to South's King, but South didn't have a Spade to return to partner. He tried a low Diamond, but West plopped down the Ace, spurning the finesse. (Declarer didn't believe in taking an unnecessary finesse.) Next, he won the Heart Ace-Queen-Jack, picked up dummy's three Club winners, and collected the Heart King. He conceded a Diamond.

It took two key plays to make 3 No Trump, ducking Spades until the third round, and unblocking the Heart suit.

III. THE DUCKING PLAY

The greatest bridge player in the world can take only one trick with an Ace, but he knows how to time the capturing of that trick so that sometimes it creates other tricks for him. Also, he knows when to play his Ace to apply the brakes on a rush of tricks to the opponents. Holding back an Ace, or a big card, and refusing to take it at the first opportunity is called *ducking*. It is one of the greatest sources of wealth in bridge, second only to the finesse. It is a very exciting card play to master.

Among the miracles you can perform at the bridge table with the ducking play are: (1) gain the timing on a hand, (2) sever communications between the defenders, (3) maintain an entry to a long suit, and (4) unblock a suit. Let's analyze each.

To Gain Time

The most famous ducking play is the Bath Coup, handed down to us from 18th century whist players of fashionable Bath, England. It is a simple hold up of the Ace when the Jack and a small card are also held.

(1)   ♡ 762
♡ KQ1085   ♡ 94
♡ AJ3

(1) West leads the Heart King and a wise South ducks the trick, letting West win. If West continues into the Ace-Jack, declarer wins two tricks instead of one. If West shifts to another suit, declarer gains time. Either way, South's hold up is lucrative.

(2) ♡ A62

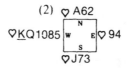

♡KQ1085   W   E ♡ 94

♡ J73

(2) Again, West leads the Heart King and South ducks. West must switch, waiting for partner to lead Hearts. If West should continue with the Queen, declarer would win the Ace and the Jack would become the ranking Heart; if West should continue with a small Heart, declarer would let it ride to the Jack. Either way South would collect two tricks.

(3) ♡ 106

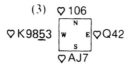

♡K98 53   W   E ♡Q42

♡AJ7

(3) Against a No Trump contract West led his fourth-best, the Heart 5, dummy followed low, and East pushed with the Queen. Declarer should win with the Ace immediately, because the lead gave him an extra trick. His 10 can smoke out the King, making the Jack boss of the suit. Don't duck when the lead gives you a trick.

To Sever Communications

You're South at 3 No Trump, and the opponents stabbed your Achilles heel on their very first play with a small Heart:

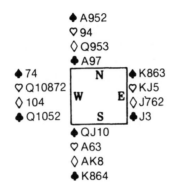

	♠ A952
	♡ 94
	◊ Q953
	♣ A97

♠ 74		♠ K863
♡ Q10872		♡ KJ5
◊ 104		◊ J762
♣ Q1052		♣ J3

	♠ QJ10
	♡ A63
	◊ AK8
	♣ K864

You have seven tricks off the top — one Spade, one Heart, three Diamonds, and two Clubs. You can bring in two or three more depending on the location of the Spade King. There is a danger you may not make them in time. The defenders may set you before you can collect your winners. If West has the Spade King you're safe; you can finesse him out of it. If East has it and returns a Heart you're in trouble. Is there anything you can do? *YES*.

If you can strip East or West of Hearts, you will stop the traffic between them and you'll have only one dangerous opponent. Hold back your Ace of Hearts as long as possible. Then, if East holds the Spade King, he'll win it, but he won't be able to return a Heart to his partner if he started with only three. So, you duck the first round and the Heart King wins; then duck the second round and let the Heart Jack take it. On the third round play your Ace. Now lead the Spade

Queen and let it ride; East takes the King but is helpless. He's out of Hearts. He can't get to partner's winners. You used the ducking play to sever communications between the defenders.

To Preserve an Entry

Now let's consider Miracle No. 3. Declarer can also use the duck to maintain communications between his hand and dummy's. Here the object is to use up one round of the opponents' cards, eliminating one card from each hand, hoping at the propitious moment all their cards in that suit will fall, promoting your little cards into winners. Here's an illustration in the most elementary form:

$\Diamond$ AK762

$\Diamond$ 543

You're South in 3 No Trump. When the dummy came down you saw you were dealt two tricks in the Diamond suit, but you need four to bring in your contract. A further complication, your only entries to dummy are the Diamond Ace and King.

It is possible to get four Diamond tricks. There are five cards out against you and they are very imposing ones, QJ1098. How are they divided in the East-West hands? There are three possible ways — 3-2, 4-1, or 5-0. If they are 3-2, the most likely division, you will have to lose only one round of Diamonds. *But it is very important which round.* If you take the Ace first, then the King, and then lose the third round you will have stripped your hand of Diamonds and have no entry to the two little ones in dummy now developed into trick-takers. It's not much good to have winners if you can't reach them.

However, if you concede the losing round first and then take your Ace and King on the second and third rounds, all the outstanding Diamonds fall and you're in dummy ready to collect those two beautiful winners.

You had to play the outstanding cards to be divided 3-2 because you had to have four tricks. Suppose, however, you didn't get to 3 No Trump; you wound up in 2 No Trump. Now you need only three Diamond tricks and you can afford to increase your chances for success. You can play for the outstanding cards to be divided 3-2 and 4-1. You can give up two rounds of Diamonds, ducking twice, and still have a little Diamond left in your hand to get to dummy's King, win the Ace, and one small Diamond. Thus sometimes ducking is used for greater safety.

The important thing is to bring in the contract. Greed for an extra trick, only 30 points and it's above the line, has lost many contracts. Don't gamble for 30 and sacrifice 70. Whenever giving up a trick enhances the chance to land a contract, the expert is happy to do so. That's how he became an expert. Suppose those cards were divided:

◊ A6543

◊ K72

Again, there's no entry to dummy except in this suit. First play the King, next give up one round, and then play the 7 to the Ace. You gave up a trick you were going to lose anyway and held onto an entry. The long suit in dummy was your prize.

Here's a gloomy picture but there's a semblance of hope:

◇ A6543

◇ 872

You have one trick but if you don't land three you're down. The Diamond Ace again is your only entry to the board. You lose the first and the second round — a double duck — and save your Ace until the third round when it's possible it will bring in the last outstanding Diamond at the strategic moment, the moment when the last two Diamonds in dummy have become winners. You don't know how the cards are distributed. You try it because you have a chance if the cards against you are divided 3-2.

The Ace will win only one trick but it makes all the difference whether it wins *before* or *after* the suit is established.

The expert player leads a dangerous life. Sometimes he has to gamble a sure winner hoping to bring in others. Unfortunately, if he loses the gamble, he may never get any tricks in that suit at all. Here's an example:

◇ AQ762

◇ 54

The perilous contract hinges on the expert finding three Diamond tricks. The only way the cards can be divided to accomplish this is for the distribution to be 3-3 and for West to hold the King. The expert plays the 4 and ducks in dummy. The next time he leads the 5 and finesses the Queen. The gamble is a possible four tricks vs. none.

Ducking to Unblock

Establishing a suit is not a great problem once you get the vision of the strategic nature of the ducking play. A big obstacle, however, is when a delicacy is needed to handle communications between you and your dummy. Sometimes you have to give up a trick that belongs to you to manipulate an entry to your long runnable suit. A strange play to call a miracle! Look:

♣ A9764

♣ QJ10

Again, we find no outside entry to dummy. When you led the Club Queen West covered with the King. Your first impulse is to win the Ace. Excitedly you see you now have no losers in the Club suit. Warning: danger ahead. Aces were made to capture Kings *when it's to your advantage*. If you put the Ace on the King you'd win the trick and you'd never, never lose a Club trick. However, something more costly would happen. After you played the Ace, you'd lead another Club and the 10 would win, then the Jack would take the third round. Now, you have two winners on the table but no access to them. You're going to take only three Club tricks.

Let's go back and play it over. Duck, let the King win. This unblocks the suit. Now when you regain the lead, play the Jack, then lead the 10 to the Ace, and you remain in dummy to cash two more Clubs. You kept communications open to the longer holding. Another way it might happen:

♣ A9764

♣ QJ2

When you led the Queen the King came tumbling down. Refuse to win the trick. If the suit breaks evenly you can rake in four tricks if you have an entry. The Ace is your entry. Give the trick to West but hold on to your entry. Later you'll take the Jack and play your 2 to the Ace and your long suit in dummy. It might happen another way:

♠ A9764

♠ KJ10

You lay down the King and everyone follows. Next you play the Jack and West covers with the Queen. Stop. Look. Suppose you win the Ace, then the 10 is the master card but it will block the suit and shut you out of dummy. Duck to unblock.

Just a note of warning. You hold up when you have a *reason;* when you don't have a reason, play your big card.

Declarer should not duck when:

- He has enough tricks and can run with them.
- Another suit is more dangerous.
- The lead has set up a trick for him.
- He can block the enemy's suit by winning.

Defenders Can Duck Too

This ducking play, so sweet to the expert declarer, can be used with equal cunning by the defenders. It is more difficult to execute because it takes perfect card play by *two* people.

The defenders can sometimes kill a long suit in dummy by ducking until declarer plays his last card in the suit.

♠ KQJ109

♠ A53

Here you are East, defending against South's 3 No Trump contract. South thinks he has four Club winners in dummy. He has no other entry. On the first lead of the suit the beginner will grab his Ace immediately. He can win the trick, why not? But the experienced player will hold up the Ace as long as he can to thwart South. If South has only three Clubs, East can destroy access to dummy's long suit.

If South had only two Clubs, East could win the Ace on the second round, killing the dummy at the precise moment to hold declarer to a minimum. In the Signaling Chapter you will learn how West can tell his partner exactly when to win the Ace.

Sometimes the defenders, too, have to give up a couple of rounds to maintain an entry to a long suit.

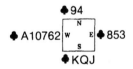
♠ 94

♠ A10762   ♠ 853

♠ KQJ

Now West has a long suit and no outside entry. Against South's 3 No Trump contract West opened his fourth best Club. Declarer won the Jack, and lost the next trick, a Heart, to East. East returned a Club and declarer put up the Queen. West refused the trick, hoping partner had one more Club and one more entry. If he had covered the Queen with the Ace he'd give up all hope of bringing in his long suit. There is an exception — if it were the setting trick West should seize the Ace.

III. Test Your Ducking Plays

1.

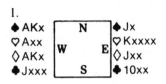

♠ AKx
♡ Axx
◇ AKx
♣ Jxxx

♠ Jx
♡ Kxxxx
◇ Jxx
♣ 10xx

West is in 2 No Trump. North leads a Spade and declarer wins the King. What cards should West play at trick two? Trick three?

2.

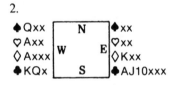

♠ Qxx
♡ Axx
◇ Axxx
♣ KQx

♠ xx
♡ xx
◇ Kxx
♣ AJ10xxx

West is playing 3 No Trump. North leads a baby Heart and South climbs up with the Queen. What card should West play? Why?

3.

♠ xx
♡ xxx
◇ AJ10987
♣ AJ

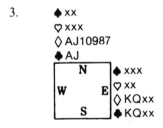

♠ xxx
♡ xx
◇ KQxx
♣ KQxx

Against South's 3 No Trump West leads the Heart Queen. Declarer wins and leads a small Diamond. East plays the King; what should he return?

4.
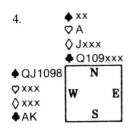

Against 3 No Trump by South West leads the Spade Queen. Declarer wins the King and leads a Club. West wins with the King. What card should he play?

5.
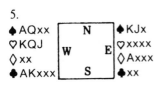

West is playing 3 No Trump; North opens the Diamond King. What card should declarer play from dummy? Why?

6.
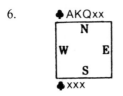

With no other entry to North's hand how does South play this card combination if he needs five tricks? If he only needs four tricks?

9. Cut Communications

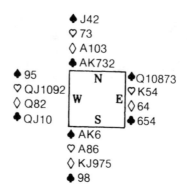

```
                        ♠ J42
                        ♡ 73
                        ◇ A103
                        ♣ AK732
        ♠ 95          ┌─────────┐    ♠ Q10873
        ♡ QJ1092      │    N    │    ♡ K54
        ◇ Q82         │ W     E │    ◇ 64
        ♣ QJ10        │    S    │    ♣ 654
                      └─────────┘
                        ♠ AK6
                        ♡ A86
                        ◇ KJ975
                        ♣ 98
```

East deals

The bidding:

East	South	West	North
Pass	1 Diamond	Pass	2 Clubs
Pass	2 No Trump	Pass	3 No Trump

Lead, Heart Queen

South opened with a Diamond and North responded 2 Clubs. Seeing all suits protected, South moved toward game in the right direction with 2 No Trump. North cheerfully called 3 No Trump.

West led the Heart Queen. South analyzed his prospects — two Spade tricks, one Heart, two Diamonds, and two Clubs, making seven. He decided Diamonds were the richest source for the other two.

Sensitive to the Heart danger, declarer ducked. West continued the Heart Jack, East threw his King on it (to unblock the suit), and again declarer declined to win. East continued a third round of Hearts and declarer took the Ace.

Poised to play Diamonds, South saw he could finesse either way, so he led the 9 and let it ride into his non-dangerous, right-hand opponent. The 9 won. Next he led toward dummy's Diamond 10, and it won. He laid down the Diamond Ace and the Queen capitulated. To get back to his hand he played a Spade to the King, and collected the other two Diamonds. Meanwhile, West was discarding high Hearts. Declarer cashed the Spade Ace and the Ace-King of Clubs. The last trick went to West's Club Queen. South scored 10 tricks.

If East happened to be the opponent with the Diamond Queen, he would capture the first Diamond trick, but since he was out of Hearts he couldn't reach partner. No matter which suit he led South could win, cash Diamond winners, and bring in the contract.

There were two key plays — ducking Hearts twice and finessing into the non-dangerous opponent.

10. Ducking To Unblock

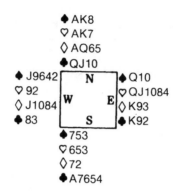

```
              ♠ AK8
              ♡ AK7
              ◇ AQ65
              ♣ QJ10
  ♠ J9642    ┌─────────┐   ♠ Q10
  ♡ 92       │    N    │   ♡ QJ1084
  ◇ J1084    │ W     E │   ◇ K93
  ♣ 83       │    S    │   ♣ K92
             └─────────┘
              ♠ 753
              ♡ 653
              ◇ 72
              ♣ A7654
```

South deals

The bidding:

South	West	North	East
Pass	Pass	2 NT	Pass
3 NT	All Pass		

Lead, Heart Queen

East opened the Heart Queen and North paused to count winners — two Spades, two Hearts, one Diamond, and two Clubs. Searching for two more he studied the suits, one at a time. The Clubs looked the friendliest, but to bring in the suit he foresaw a problem — the Club Ace was the only entry.

North won the Heart King and switched to the Queen of Clubs. East topped it with the King and declarer pulled a low card from dummy, permitting the King to win. Surprised, East grabbed the trick. (Dummy bit his lip.) East pursued with the Heart Jack and declarer went up with the Ace. North played the Club Jack, all following; then he led the Club 10, overtaking with dummy's Ace. Then, he led the Club 7 and 6, both winners. He played to his Diamond Ace, declining to finesse, and collected his high Spades. He conceded the rest, making 3 No Trump.

"A fascinating play, partner," said South, applauding. "Now I understand why you gave East his Club King. You had to save the Ace for the third round to reach those extra winners." Leaning back in his chair, North beamed.

11. Bridge Is for the Brave

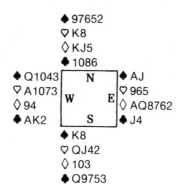

```
            ♠ 97652
            ♡ K8
            ◇ KJ5
            ♣ 1086
♠ Q1043    ┌─────────┐    ♠ AJ
♡ A1073    │    N    │    ♡ 965
◇ 94       │ W     E │    ◇ AQ8762
♣ AK2      │    S    │    ♣ J4
           └─────────┘
            ♠ K8
            ♡ QJ42
            ◇ 103
            ♣ Q9753
```

West deals

The bidding:

West	North	East	South
1 Club	Pass	1 Diamond	Pass
1 Heart	Pass	3 Diamonds	Pass
3 No Trump	All Pass		

Lead, Spade 5

St. Elizabeth's Hospital in Washington, D.C., developed a bridge program which became so successful with the patients that the hospital arranged instruction for the staff to provide the doctors with an extra line of communication. One day Dr. George Saiger, a psychiatrist, dealt himself the West hand and ended up in a perilous 3 No Trump contract.

North led his fourth best Spade, and declarer played the Jack from dummy. But South won the King and returned a Spade, knocking out dummy's only outside entry to the long Diamonds. The good doctor could count only seven tricks

— three Spades, one Heart, one Diamond, and two Clubs. He diagnosed that only the Diamonds could rescue his contract.

He pulled a low Diamond from dummy and North won the Jack. North continued with the Spade 9 and declarer won with his 10. Now the young psychiartrist led his last Diamond, North played low, and the doctor risked his Diamond Queen. It held! He was home! The Ace brought in the King, and there were three small Diamonds to bring in three more tricks. Then he collected his Heart Ace, top Spade, and two big Clubs to score 11 tricks.

Landing his contract required two key plays, the duck and the finesse. His technique was good, his courage excellent — both valuable attributes, also, for a psychiatrist working in St. Elizabeth's maximum security wards.

12. A 100% Play

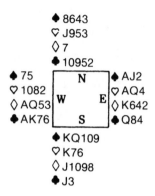

North deals

The bidding:

North	East	South	West
Pass	1 NT	Pass	3 NT
All Pass			

Lead, Spade King

South led the Spade King, top of an imperfect sequence. Declarer assessed eight ready-made tricks and saw several sources for the ninth — the Diamonds might break 3-2, the Clubs might break 3-3, the Hearts might be finessed, or he might make the Spade Jack.

He played a low Spade at trick one. Fearing the Bath Coup, South shifted to the Diamond Jack, which rode to the King.

Declarer ran three Clubs but South failed to follow on the last one. Then he pulled the Diamond Ace, and learned they were banked in the South hand. Should he try the Heart finesse, he asked himself. It was a 50% chance for a trick. Suddenly, he realized he had a 100% play. He saw a way to get South to lead them for him! Declarer won the Diamond Queen, and then gave South his high Diamond.

South had just become the victim of an end play. This was the situation:

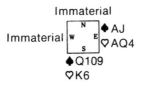

Immaterial

Immaterial ♠AJ
♡AQ4

♠Q109
♡K6

What could poor South do? Lead Hearts or Spades? Helpless, he laid down a Heart, donating East his ninth trick.

IV. THE POINT-COUNT SYSTEM

Once upon a time Charles J. Solomon, prominent player and author, opened 1 Spade holding ♠AKxxx ♡A ♢Jxxx ♣KQx, and the bidding proceeded — Pass, Pass, Pass. After the opening lead his partner laid down the dummy, ♠Qxxxx ♡xxxx ♢--- ♣xxxx.

"Partner," declarer demanded, "why didn't you give me a raise?"

"I only had two points."

Gesturing at the Diamond void, Solomon indignantly retorted, "Why you have the Ace-King-Queen of Diamonds!" Solomon sailed off with 11 tricks.

Simply using common sense Solomon's partner should have seen that he had two to four tricks and given Solomon a boost. He must have learned only the fundamental point-count table:

Ace	= 4	Void	= 3
King	= 3	Singleton	= 2
Queen	= 2	Doubleton	= 1
Jack	= 1		

The pack contains 40 points.
An average hand is 10.

However, there is a great deal more to the point-count system. It can help you uncover hidden values and warn you of weaknesses.

Holding all four Aces, add a point because it's strategically valuable to be able to win the first trick no matter what is led. Conversely, the opener with no Aces subtracts one point.

An unprotected honor is a flaw, so subtract a point holding a King alone, Queen alone, Jack alone, Queen doubleton, or Jack doubleton.

Give yourself an extra point for good "body cards" — 9's and 10's. They are pushers and sometimes they take tricks.

Look what a 10 does to these combinations:

AQ2 - 50% chance for two tricks
AQ10 - 75% chance for two tricks

AJ2 - 25% chance for two tricks
AJ10 - 75% chance for two tricks

KJ3 - 75% chance for one trick
KJ10 - always one trick, 50% chance for two

Where Are Your Honors?

When your honors are in your long suit, they are more valuable.

♠AQ1052 ♡AK3 ◊1087 ♣53

is worth more than

♠108752 ♡AK3 ◊1087 ♣AQ

When your honors are together, they're more likely to produce tricks. In the hand above, you have a right to expect two Heart tricks, but separate your Ace and King:

♠108752 ♡A83 ◊K107 ♣AQ

and you'll win the Ace and *maybe* the King.

Some Points Are Better than Others

Aces and Kings are more important than Queens and Jacks. Queens and Jacks have to wait to be set up and, by then, might get trumped. A couple of Jacks without supporting cards may be useless.

Beware of counting too much for distributional points until a satisfactory trump suit is found.

Re-evaluation by the Opener

Sometimes the bidding will change your attitude toward your points. The expert adjusts his evaluation as the bidding progresses.

♠AQ3 ♡AQ10432 ◇76 ♣54

Here you have 12 high-card points plus 2 distributional points so you open 1 Heart. Your partner gives you a single raise to 2 Hearts, and your right-hand opponent overcalls 2 Spades. Now study your hand. The bidding has turned it into a thing of beauty.

The Spades are no longer six points. East says he has a strong enough Spade holding to come in at the two level. He practically said, "I have the King of Spades." What is the opening lead going to be? A Spade, you can be sure. You are going to finesse that King on the first trick. Your AQ is as good as an AK. Count it seven points.

Usually you rate your cards a trifle higher when your right-hand opponent bids because your finesses are more likely to work; conversely, when your left-hand opponent bids, a trifle lower. Avoid attributing any points to an unprotected honor in a suit your opponents bid except as a singleton or doubleton.

When your partner raised your Hearts, he said he had three or more cards in the Heart suit. You're going to be able to lead the enemy out of trumps in two or three rounds. Your fifth and sixth cards in the suit are no longer a lowly 3 and 2. They're winners. They're going to take tricks. **So, re-evaluate**

your trumps. Take an extra point for your fifth trump and two extra points for each additional trump.

Re-evaluated, your values are:

Spades 7, Hearts 6 + 3, Diamonds 1, and Clubs 1 = 18.

Suddenly, you like your hand! Bid 3 Hearts inviting your partner to bid game if he is on the top of his raise.

Dummy Points

The responder also adjusts his points as the bidding proceeds. An honor in partner's suit is more valuable than the same honor would be in any other suit, so give it VIP treatment — **add one point to one trump honor, making a King 4, a Queen 3, or a Jack 2. However, don't promote any if you already have four points in the suit** (don't promote an Ace). Here's an example:

♠x ♡Kxxx ◊Kxxx ♣xxxx

It doesn't look like much but that depends on the bidding. Partner opened 1 Heart. A trump suit has been discovered! Promote the Heart King to 4 points.

A short suit in the Dummy is more valuable because the declarer can make extra tricks by trumping with dummy's trumps (saving his own to pull the enemy's), so dummy gets extra for short suits:

Void	= **5**
Singleton	= **3**
Doubleton	= **1**

Now add the values — Heart King = 4. Diamond King = 3, Singleton = 3.

You have a count of 10 and cheerfully raise to 2 Hearts. If partner happens to invite you to contract for game, you will accept and bid 4 Hearts. Suppose, however, your left-hand opponent overcalled Diamonds.

Partner	West	You	East
1 Heart	Pass	2 Hearts	3 Diamonds
3 Hearts	Pass	?	

How would you feel about your hand? You don't like it anymore. The King of Diamonds is going to be finessed on the opening lead; it looks like a dead card. The bidding cut your values to 7 points. Decline that invitation. Pass.

Let's rearrange those cards another way and, again, partner opens 1 Heart:

♠xxx ♡Kxxx ♢xxx ♣Kxx

On this hand you have even distribution. **It's a flaw for a dummy to be unable to trump.** Subtract one point, leaving only six points. You barely eke out a raise to 2 Hearts.

The point-count system and your common sense are a marvelous combination at the bridge table.

At all times keep in mind:

- 26 points will usually make 3NT, 4♡ or 4♠
- 29 points will usually make 5♣ or 5♢
- 33 points will usually make a small slam
- 37 points will usually make a grand slam

Tip

• There is an argument among bridge players about how good a 16-point hand is — whether it is a minimum hand and belongs with 13-15, or is a medium hand and belongs with 17-18. Experienced bridge players frequently say, "I had only 16 points but I liked my hand" or "I had 16 points but I didn't like my hand." These factors would affect your judgment of the value of a hand, helping you decide whether a borderline hand belongs in one category or the next. Example, You - 1♡ , Partner - 2♡ , You - ?

	(1)	♠KJ4	(2)	♠KQJ
		♡Q8762		♡AK1094
		◊KJ2		◊J109
		♣A4		♣32

Both hands re-evaluate at 16 points, but (1) is a poor hand with no touching honors, no "body", and the high cards aren't in the long suit. Pass. (2) is a good hand, bid 3 Hearts to invite a game.

• When bidding No Trump, count only high cards, don't deduct for an unsupported honor, and give yourself an extra point for a five-card suit containing two honors.

Point-Count Summary

All four Aces +1
Unprotected honor –1
Two five-card suits +1
Promote Kings and
    Queens if right-hand
    opponent bids suit;
    demote if left-hand
    opponent bids

Good "body" +1
Honor in partner's suit +1
    (unless already have
    four in suit)
Fifth trump +1, each
    additional +2 (after
    trump suit is found)

Opener

Void +3
Singleton +2
Doubleton +1
No Aces –1

Dummy

Void +5
Singleton +3
Doubleton +1
Even distribution –1
Only three trumps –1

IV. Test Your Point-Counting

Calculate the point-count and make your opening bid on:

(1)	♠ KQ4	(2)	♠ 109864	(3)	♠ KJ86432	(4)	♠ KQ3
	♡ K532		♡ AKQJ		♡ 92		♡ AQ42
	◊ KJ9		◊ 32		◊ AK		◊ J32
	♣ J96		♣ A2		♣ 84		♣ K87

The bidding has gone

	You	**Partner**
	1♠	2♠
	?	

Re-evaluate, give point-count and make your rebid:

(5)	♠ AJ864	(6)	♠ AK8654	(7)	♠ AK97542
	♡ K53		♡ K75		♡ KQ6
	◊ A875		◊ K86		◊ Q92
	♣ 4		♣ 5		♣ ---

As responder, choose your next bid:

	Partner	**You**
	1♣	1♠
	2♣	?

(8)	♠ KJ865	(9)	♠ 1098765	(10)	♠ J9876
	♡ 953		♡ 8		♡ 65
	◊ 8		◊ AQJ		◊ 6
	♣ 9532		♣ 1082		♣ AKJ64

Partner opened 1 Heart; what is your point-count and response:

(11)	♠ AQ753	(12)	♠ 86	(13)	♠ AQ82	(14)	♠ 9
	♡ K642		♡ Q8532		♡ 8		♡ Q872
	◊ 7		◊ 853		◊ AK72		◊ Q862
	♣ 853		♣ 942		♣ A952		♣ 9532

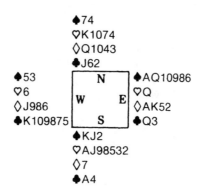

13. Those Points Can Change

South deals

The bidding:

South	West	North	East
1 Heart	Pass	2 Hearts	2 Spades
4 Hearts	Pass	Pass	Pass

South opened a Heart with 13 high-card points and a long, long suit. North gave a single raise; he promoted his trump King to four points and worked his count up to eight. Then East came in with 2 Spades. Now the opener re-evaluated his hand. The opening lead was going to be a Spade (!) and he'd get one and maybe two Spade tricks. He could see all his little Hearts would be winners and he gave himself a point for the fifth and two each for the sixth and the seventh. Now his hand was worth 21! He contracted for game.

West led the top of his doubleton, the Spade 5 and East won the Ace. He played the Diamond King, and then switched back to Spades playing the 10, the top of his internal sequence. Declarer hopped up with the King and laid down the Ace of Hearts bringing in all the outstanding trumps in one fell swoop. He led the Spade Jack, and ruffed in dummy. He played the Diamond 4 hoping East would bring out the Ace but East chose a baby Diamond and declarer ruffed. Then he ran all his trumps, hoping the opponents would discard wrong and give him a trick, but they didn't. Nevertheless, he took 10 tricks and scored a game.

14. With an Ear to the Bidding

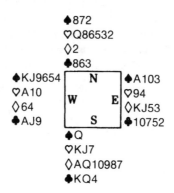

```
              ♠872
              ♡Q86532
              ◇2
              ♣863
♠KJ9654    ┌─────────┐    ♠A103
♡A10       │    N    │    ♡94
◇64        │ W     E │    ◇KJ53
♣AJ9       │    S    │    ♣10752
           └─────────┘
              ♠Q
              ♡KJ7
              ◇AQ10987
              ♣KQ4
```

West deals

The bidding:

West	North	East	South
1 Spade	Pass	2 Spades	3 Diamonds
3 Spades	All Pass		

With a minimum opener West started with 1 Spade and East, with a healthy nine points, gave a single raise. Then South interjected a Diamond overcall. West re-evaluated (13 + 2 for distribution + 3 for the extra Spades = 18) and found himself in a higher bracket. He bid 3 Spades, issuing a game invitation. East had to decline. He passed. Trading on the knowledge the Diamond honors were useless, he devalued his hand to five points.

North led the Diamond 2, declarer played dummy's Jack, and South won the Queen. South added his Diamonds to dummy's and realized there was only one outstanding Diamond. Partner couldn't have it, because he would have led the top of a doubleton. Therefore, partner started with a singleton. He returned the Diamond 7 and North ruffed. North played back a low Heart and South went up with the King, forcing declarer's Ace.

West led a low Spade to the Ace, and another back to the King, bringing in all the trumps. He exited with a Heart and North won the Queen. North switched to a Club, South pushed with the Queen, and declarer took his Ace. Declarer gave up a Club and claimed the rest, making nine on the nose.

15. Blueprint the Bidding

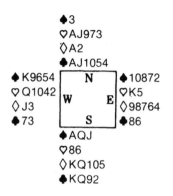

North deals

The bidding:

North	East	South	West
1 Heart	Pass	3 NT	Pass
6 Clubs	All Pass		

North opened a Heart and partner jumped to 3 No Trump showing 16-18 points and even distribution. North stopped to visualize partner's hand:

Thought 1. Partner didn't have three Hearts or he would raise; since the No Trump bid showed a balanced hand, partner held a Heart doubleton.

Thought 2. Partner skipped over the Spade suit so he didn't have four cards in that suit. Since he couldn't have another doubleton, he had specifically three Spades.

Thought 3. That leaves eight cards in the minors. They can be divided 5-3 or 4-4 and maintain even distribution. Therefore, the partnership holds either eight, nine, or ten Clubs.

Now, North re-evaluated his hand with Clubs as trumps and it soared to 18 points! His intelligent blueprint showed, "Partner's minimum 16 + my 18 = 34." He bid 6 Clubs.

East led the Diamond 9 and declarer won the Ace. He extracted trumps with the King and Queen. Pulling a small Heart from dummy, he ducked, and East won the King. East switched to the Spade deuce but declarer won the Ace (saving a no-thank-you to that finesse!) and continued a Heart to the Ace. He ruffed a Heart in dummy. He led the Spade Queen, West covered with the King (hoping to turn the setting trick), but declarer ruffed. Now he had plenty of tricks. He led a Heart and ruffed in dummy, took the Diamond King-Queen, and the Spade Jack. The closed hand was all trumps, so North claimed the rest. He brought in an even dozen.

16. Watch the "Body"

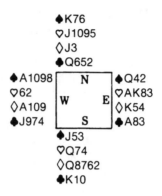

♠K76
♡J1095
◊J3
♣Q652

♠A1098   ♠Q42
♡62   ♡AK83
◊A109   ◊K54
♣J974   ♣A83

♠J53
♡Q74
◊Q8762
♣K10

East deals

The bidding:

East	South	West	North
1 NT	Pass	2 Clubs	Pass
2 Hearts	Pass	3 NT	All Pass

After East opened a No Trump, West Stayman-ed, but partner had the wrong major. Preparing to return to No Trump, West carefully counted nine high-card points, looked admiringly at his 10's and 9's, and valued his hand at 10+. He went to game.

South led the Diamond 6, covered by dummy's 9, then North's Jack, and won by declarer's King. East could count only six tricks and he had some developing to do. He felt sure he knew who held the Diamond Queen so he could finesse, probably establishing dummy's 10. Moving over to Spades, the double finesse was a 75% chance to produce two additional tricks. Hearts looked naked, but he could resort to the fractured Clubs for a last-ditch stand.

Declarer led the Spade Queen, finessing, and North won the King. North saw returning partner's Diamonds would give declarer a free finesse so he shifted to the Heart Jack. East plopped down the King, and went back to his Spades. He had this play down pat. Again, he led from his hand and finessed the 9. It won. Over to his hand via the Club Ace, he repeated the Spade finesse. When the Jack appeared he covered with the Ace and cashed the Spade 10, just promoted into a winner. Now back to his hand with the Heart Ace, he played a low Diamond and held his breath as he finessed that 10. It won. He cashed the Diamond Ace and relaxed. He had his nine tricks; North-South were welcome to the rest.

East played perfectly, but West was a hero, too. If he hadn't seen the hidden value of his 10's and 9's the partnership would have played in a partial. If he had bid only 2 NT, opener, on a minimum, would have to pass.

V. REBID BY THE OPENER

The opening bid is usually an easy choice. A novice can choose correctly almost every time. The *second* bid made by the opener is the most important bid. Here judgment begins. There are two pictures to focus on and you try to clarify both — the range of your point-count and the distribution of your cards. You choose different bids to describe different types of hands.

Point-Count Categories

When you opened one of a suit you could have as few as 13 points or as many as 21. This next bid narrows that range. First, re-evaluate your hand in case the bidding raised or lowered your values. Then, you can choose a rebid that limits your strength to a three-point span if you rebid No Trumps, raise your partner's suit, or rebid your original suit. Since these present such a precise picture, they are called "limit bids". They reveal whether you had:

- Minimum opener of 13-15
- Medium opener of 16-18
- Maximum opener of 19-21

When your rebid is in a new suit — you're still searching for the best contract — the picture is not as clear. You name the suit at the lowest level if you have a minimum or a medium hand. You skip a level, make a jump-shift, with a maximum.

Distribution Categories

Your rebid also discloses more about your hand pattern. It describes:

- Even distribution. lending itself to No Trump, or
- Uneven distribution, better for suit play —
  One long suit, six or more cards
  Two possible trump suits, 5-5 or 5-4
  Three possible trump suits, 5-4-4-0 or 4-4-4-1

A Minimum Opener 13-15

The way to tell your partner you opened the bidding with a minimum is to pass if you can. You have shown an opening bid and you don't have any more. There's no use to bid again unless partner makes a forcing bid.

If partner offers a single raise (You-1♡ , Partner-2♡) he has 6-9 "dummy points". The magic game number of 26 is out of reach. Naturally, you pass.

If partner responds 1 No Trump (You-1♡ , Partner-1 NT), pass unless your hand is unsuitable for No Trump play. With an unbalanced hand and six or more cards in your original suit, rebid your suit at the lowest level. With two possible trump suits, name your other suit if it is lower in rank than your first suit. (You-1♡ , Partner-1 NT, You-2◊ or 2♠ .)

If partner names a new suit it is forcing and you *must* speak again, but do so at the lowest level possible:

- Give partner a single raise with adequate trump support
- Rebid your original suit with six cards
- Name a new suit at the 1-level (You-1♠ , Partner-1◊ , You-1 ♡), or at the 2-level if the suit is lower in rank than your first suit. (You-1◊, Partner 1♠ , You-2♠)

- Rebid 1 No Trump with even distribution (You-1♡, Partner-1♠, You-1 NT)

Let's practice. You opened 1 Heart and Partner responded 1 Spade. What's your rebid on these:

(1) ♠Q2 (2) ♠x (3) ♠Jxxx (4) ♠xx
♡AJxxx ♡AQxxx ♡KQ10xx ♡AJ9xxx
◇Axx ◇AQx ◇xx ◇xx
♣QJx ♣J10xx ♣AQ ♣AQJ

(1) Rebid 1 No Trump with even distribution. (2) Your suit isn't strong enough to rebid; you don't want to bid a No Trump with a singleton. The only bid available is 2 Clubs. Your Diamonds are more attractive but, if your second suit winds up being trumps, quantity is more important than quality. (3) You have Spade support and a minimum; bid 2 Spades. (4) You can rebid your six-card suit, say 2 Hearts.

A Medium Opener 16-18

The medium hand is the range of an opening 1 No Trump; that is the wisest opening bid because it tells the whole story at once. An auction that begins with a No Trump is generally easy and accurate. However, when you have a hand with uneven distribution or a long major, you open one of a suit.

This is the same opening bid you would make with a minimum hand, so you try to show the difference at your next opportunity to bid by choosing an encouraging bid, by issuing a game invitation of some sort.

If partner gave a single raise of your major, there is hope for game. Show your extra points by inviting game. You - 1♡, Partner - 2♡, You - 3♡. This asks partner to carry on if he is on the top of his raise. Another way to make a game-try is to bid a new suit. This is a more specific way to issue a game invitation. You - 1♡, Partner - 2♡, You - 3♣.

You are telling partner you want to be in game if he can take care of some Club losers. If he can help you in this second suit, he bids 4 Hearts; if he can't, he retreats to 3 Hearts. The Club bid is forcing because you've already agreed to play a Heart contract.

If partner responds 1 No Trump, and you have even distribution, invite game by bidding 2 No Trump. With uneven distribution and a six-card suit, jump one level in your suit. You - 1♡ , Partner - 1 NT, You - 3♡ . This shows a good suit like AQJxxx or AJ109xx. With two possible trump suits, name your second suit if it is lower in rank than your first. Do not skip a level. Remember, this rebid is the same for a medium or a minimum hand. *It's the only rebid that doesn't fit into a separate slot.*

Here are some examples. You - 1♡ , Partner - 1♠ . What's your next bid?

(1) ♠x	(2) ♠Qx	(3) ♠Qxxx	(4) ♠Kx
♡AKxxx	♡AKJ9xx	♡QJ10xx	♡AQxxx
◊AKxx	◊AQx	◊---	◊x
♣Qxx	♣xx	♣AQJ10	♣AJ10xx

(1) Rebid 2 Diamonds offering another possible trump suit. (2) Jump to 3 Hearts to show your extra trump. (3) Re-evaluated as a dummy, you have 18; give partner a jump raise to 3 Spades. Don't be seduced into bidding Clubs. A trump suit has been found; make the glorious announcement. (4) Rebid your second suit, 2 Clubs.

A Maximum Opener 19-21

With 19-21 you open one of a suit. There isn't a way to show on your first bid you have the maximum holding. However, if partner responds, there should be a game somewhere. A *jump* rebid of some kind is prescribed.

If partner gives a single raise of your major (You - 1♡, Partner - 2♡) you see game. GO. *Jump to game.* Bid 4 Hearts.

If partner bids a new suit, a major (You - 1♡, Partner 1♠), and you have four-card support, show your values with an immediate *jump to game.* Bid 4 Spades.

If you have even distribution your hand is too big to open a No Trump. On your rebid, with 19 *jump* to 2 No Trump, and with 20 or 21 *jump* to 3 No Trump. What if partner's response was 1 No Trump? Add your points to his. Jump to 3 No Trump.

Suppose you have uneven distribution with two possible trump suits. You have 10 red cards, five Hearts and five Diamonds. Make a *jump-shift* to 3 Diamonds; this forces partner to bid again. You - 1♡, Partner - 1♠, You 3◊.

If you have a long, self-sustaining major, AKJ10xxx, jump to game. You - 1♡, Partner - 1♠, You - 4♡. If you had a long six-card suit but it wasn't strong enough to play opposite a void or a singleton in dummy, AQ9xxx, you have a problem. Holding ♠ xx ♡ A109xxx ◊ AQ ♣ AKQ, you will have to be resourceful. Manufacture a bid. Make a *jump-shift* to 3 Clubs. Whenever you have to tell your partner a lie about your hand make it about your distribution; don't lie about your point-count.

With a maximum you can rebid a new suit at the 2-level even if it is higher ranking than your first suit. You - 1♡, Partner - 1 NT, You - 2♠. It's called a "reverse" and is forcing. Partner must bid again. If he prefers your first suit, he has to acknowledge it at the 3-level, pushing the bidding very high. You need a strong, maximum hand to do that.

Try rebidding a maximum on these. You - 1♡, Partner - 1♠:

(1) ♠Axxx (2) ♠Qx (3) ♠Kx (4) ♠xx
    ♡KQJxx   ♡Axxxx   ♡KJ10xx   ♡AKJ10xxx
    ◊AQ10x   ◊AKx   ◊Axx   ◊Kx
    ♣---   ♣KQJ   ♣AKQ   ♣AK

(1) Re-evaluated you have 21. Bid 4 Spades. When the opener sees game he bids it. (2) With even distribution and 19 points jump to 2 No Trump. (3) With even distribution and 20 points jump to 3 No Trump. (4) Your Hearts are strong enough to play even with a void in dummy. You have no interest in any other trump suit. Jump to 4 Hearts.

Rebids by Opener

13-15

Pass if partner gave a single raise

Raise partner 1 with trump support

Rebid your original suit with six cards

Name a new suit, 1-level

Name a new suit, 2-level, lower in rank

Rebid 1 NT with balanced hand

16-18

Bid 3 if partner gave single raise

Jump raise partner with trump support

Jump your original suit with six cards

Name a new suit, 1-level

Name a new suit, 2-level, lower in rank

If partner responded 1 NT, bid 2 NT with even distribution

19-21

Bid 4 if partner gave a single raise

Jump partner to game with trump support

Jump to game in original suit if self sustaining

Jump-shift in new suit

Reverse in new suit, forcing

Jump to 2 NT with 19, balanced hand

Jump to 3 NT with 20 or 21, balanced hand

V. Test Your Rebids as the Opening Bidder

Choose the rebid that shows your *point count* and *distribution*. For the second and third column of answers please substitute the card indicated for a little card in the same suit.

You   **Partner**

1♡ [N W E S] 1♠

?

        Add   Also add
        ♠Ace   ♠King

1. ♠AJxx ♡KQJxxx ◇10 ♣xx ____ ____ ____

2. ♠xx ♡AQJxx ◇x ♣QJxxx ____ ____ ____

3. ♠Ax ♡AKxxx ◇Qxx ♣Jxx ____ ____ ____

4. ♠Axx ♡AK109xx ◇x ♣xxx ____ ____ ____

You   **Partner**

1♡ [N W E S] 1 NT

?

        Add   Also add
        ♠Ace   ♠King

5. ♠Kxx ♡AQJxx ◇Qxx ♣xx ____ ____ ____

You   **Partner**

1♡ [N W E S] 2♣

?

        Add   Also add
        ♠Ace   ♠King

6. ♠Ax ♡AK10xx ◇xx ♣J9xx ____ ____ ____

7. ♠AKxx ♡AJ9xx ◇xx ♣xx ____ ____ ____

You   **Partner**

1♡ [N W E S] 2♡

?

        Add   Also add
        ♡King   ♠King

8. ♠xx ♡AJ10xx ◇Ax ♣Qxxx ____ ____ ____

17. Cover an Honor with an Honor

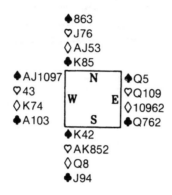

```
              ♠863
              ♡J76
              ◊AJ53
              ♣K85
  ♠AJ1097  ┌──────────┐  ♠Q5
  ♡43      │    N     │  ♡Q109
  ◊K74     │ W     E  │  ◊10962
  ♣A103    │    S     │  ♣Q762
           └──────────┘
              ♠K42
              ♡AK852
              ◊Q8
              ♣J94
```

South deals

The bidding:

South	West	North	East
1 Heart	1 Spade	2 Hearts	All Pass

South opened a Heart and West overcalled a Spade. North offered a single raise. South could see his Spade King was badly placed and there was trouble ahead. He passed.

Fearing any lead would give declarer a trick, West finally chose a low trump, and declarer won the King. South continued the Heart Ace and all followed. There was only one trump outstanding; it was a winner, so declarer didn't lead for it.

South shifted to the Diamond Queen, West covered with his King, and dummy's Ace topped it. Declarer took the Diamond Jack and continued a Diamond, ruffing in the closed hand. He led a low Club, West played low, and declarer hopped up with dummy's King, which held.

He played a Club back, and East stepped out with the Queen. He collected his high trump, pulling one from declarer and dummy. He laid down the Spade Queen, which won, then played another Spade through declarer. West won the 10 and walked out with the Ace, declarer's King crumbling under it. Now West took his Club Ace. Declarer won the last trick with a trump. He was down one.

Declarer was doomed when West covered the Diamond Queen with the King, forcing declarer to contribute two honors to one trick. If West had played low, hoarding the King, the Queen would triumph. Now South could lead toward the Ace-Jack, finessing again, and harvest three Diamond tricks. This would present him with the contract.

18. Every Hand Is Different

Contributed by Baltimore's Becky Levering

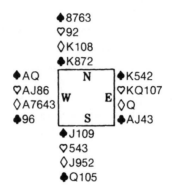

♠8763
♡92
◊K108
♣K872

♠AQ   ♠K542
♡AJ86   ♡KQ107
◊A7643 ◊Q
♣96   ♣AJ43

♠J109
♡543
◊J952
♣Q105

West deals

The bidding:

West	North	East	South
1 Diamond	Pass	1 Heart	Pass
3 Hearts	Pass	4 NT	Pass
5 Spades	Pass	6 Hearts	All Pass

In response to West's opening, East, holding four cards in each major, correctly responded 1 Heart. West's jump rebid of 3 Hearts showed four trumps and 16-18 points. Blackwooding for Aces, East landed in 6 Hearts. South found the safe opening lead of the Spade Jack.

Declarer stopped to get the lay of the land. His study revealed only ten tricks — three Spades, five Hearts, one Diamond, and one Club. That wasn't enough. With a short suit in each hand, he decided to try a cross-ruff.

East knew the secret of a cross-ruff was to play side winners first. He cashed the Ace-Queen of Spades, came to his hand with the Club Ace and took the Spade King, dropping dummy's last Club. Now the cross-ruff was ready.

Declarer led to the Diamond Ace and returned a Diamond to trump with the 7. Now a Club was ruffed with the Heart 6. A Diamond followed, ruffed with the Heart 10. A Club again to ruff with the Heart 8. Declarer breathed a sigh of relief because he was now safe from the danger of an overruff; all his trumps were high. He led a Diamond and trumped with the Heart Queen, a Club back to ruff with the Heart Jack. A Diamond ruffed with the Heart King, and finally a Club trumped with the Heart Ace. He landed all 13 tricks.

"Congratulations," said his partner, smiling proudly.

"If I had drawn trumps," explained East, "I would have gone down two."

19. Make a Game Plan at Trick One

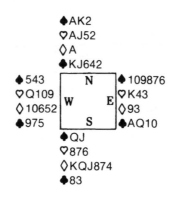

♠AK2
♡AJ52
◊A
♣KJ642

♠543　　　　　♠109876
♡Q109　　　　♡K43
◊10652　　　◊93
♣975　　　　　♣AQ10

♠QJ
♡876
◊KQJ874
♣83

North deals

The bidding:

North	East	South	West
1 Club	Pass	1 Diamond	Pass
2 Hearts	Pass	3 Diamonds	Pass
3 NT	All Pass		

North opened a Club and partner responded 1 Diamond. With 20 highs North made a jump-shift to 2 Hearts, guaranteeing another chance to bid. South could only reiterate Diamonds so North settled in 3 No Trump.

East led the Spade 10. Declarer immediately spied six Diamond tricks and focused on how to collect them. His Ace singleton locked him out of dummy. After a moment's concentration he pulled dummy's lowest Spade, the Jack, a winner, but meticulously overtook it with the Spade King. Then he plopped down the Diamond Ace. Now he played the carefully preserved Spade 2 over to the Spade Queen. He ran dummy's five winning Diamonds, discarding from the closed hand three Hearts and two Clubs.

Declarer led a Club from dummy, finessing the Jack, but East was ready with the Queen. East returned a Heart and North won the Ace, took the Spade Ace, and bowed out. East brought in the last two tricks with the Heart King and the Club Ace. North emerged with 10 tricks.

Without North's key play at trick one the whole edifice would have crumbled. Overtaking the Spade Jack with the King cost nothing; he always had three Spade tricks and he would still get three. That strategic play allowed dummy to win the second round instead of the first, saving an entry to the Diamonds. Declarer was well rewarded for his perspicacity with dummy's five Diamond tricks.

20. The End Play Was 100%

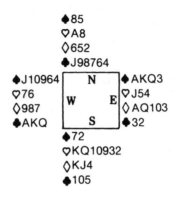

East deals

The bidding:

East	South	West	North
1 Diamond	1 Heart	1 Spade	Pass
3 Spades	Pass	4 Spades	All Pass

East wisely bid 1 Diamond. He had even distribution and 16 high's, but only two suits protected, too risky for No Trump. South overcalled a Heart and West introduced Spades. East, holding 17, offered a jump raise, and West bid game.

North opened the Heart Ace, continued another, and South won the Queen. Next, he played the Heart King. Declarer held a wealth of big Spades and climbed up with the Jack of trumps, winning. He extracted the opponents' trumps with two leads. Then declarer collected the Club Ace-King-Queen, on the last discarding a little Diamond from dummy.

At this propitious moment, he led a Diamond, inserted dummy's 10, and South won the Jack. The defenders were book-in. South started squirming in his chair, and scowling at his cards; he had just become the victim of an "end play". This was the situation:

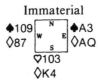

Immaterial

♠109 ♠A3
♢87 ♢AQ
♡103
♢K4

A player is end-played when he has to lead and any card he chooses costs his side a trick. If South returned a Diamond, he had to lead into the teeth of dummy's AQ. If he led a Heart, declarer could get a ruff and a sluff. Helpless, South finally pulled a Heart. Declarer discarded a losing Diamond from his hand while he ruffed in dummy. He led the Diamond Ace, then followed with the Diamond Queen, covered by South's King, and trumped in the closed hand. He claimed the rest, eking out his game contract.

One of the first things we learn in bridge is how to finesse. A player must understand finessing before he can understand when another play is better. Throughout this hand West worried about losing two Diamonds. He knew the double finesse was a 75% play but he feared the losing 25% might be operating today. The bidding clearly indicated South had the King; if he also had the Jack he could sink the contract. West found a better play — a 100% play — when he stripped South of Clubs and Spades, and then threw him in with a Diamond, leaving no safe exit card. The clever play made everyone happy, everyone except North and South.

VI. RESPONDER'S REBID

When your partner opened the bidding he launched your partnership on a journey. How far are you going? To a part-score, a game, or a slam? Your mission is to guide the auction, keeping it short and simple, avoiding an unnecessary detour. Lengthy bidding sequences increase the chance one player or the other will lose his way.

At the moment of your first response decide how many bids you intend to take:

- bid once with 6-9 points (occasionally 10) unless partner asks you a question
- make two forward-going bids with 10-12
- reach a game with 13-15
- show slam interest with 16-18, but shy away if partner applies the brakes with minimum rebids
- flash a slam signal with 19 or more

Did you notice all of these span three points? When you learn one, the others follow logically in order.

With 6-9 Points

The responder's rebid is simple if the first response was a single raise, 1♡ — 2♡. Any further bid by the opener, short of game, invites you to bid a game.

(1) **Partner**   **You**
    1♡   2♡
    3♡   ?

(2) **Partner**   **You**
    1♡   2♡
    3♢   ?

(1) Partner is asking you to go to game if you are on the top of your raise. With a scant 6 or 7, pass. With 8, think

about accepting. With 9, accept the invitation, bid 4 Hearts. Partner's hand is something like ♠AJx ♡AQxxx ♢xx ♣Axx.

(2) Another way the opener can show interest in game is to bid a new suit. This is a special way to make a game-try, based specifically on your holding in the second suit. Here partner said, "If you have help in Diamonds, I have a chance to make a game. Can you take care of some Diamond losers?" With the Ace, the King, or the Queen-Jack, a singleton, or a void, go to game. Otherwise, sign off with 3 Hearts. Partner's Diamond bid is forcing; both of you have agreed to play Hearts. Partner's hand might be ♠xx ♡AQJxx ♢AJxxx ♣x.

Try these examples, counting dummy points. Partner 1♡, You - 2♡, Partner - 3♡, You - ?

(1) ♠Qx	(2) ♠xxx	(3) ♠109xx	(4) ♠Ax
♡K9xx	♡K9xx	♡109xx	♡10xxx
♢Kxxx	♢KJx	♢x	♢xxx
♣xxx	♣xxx	♣AJ10x	♣KJxx

(1) You have 9. Accept. Bid 4 Hearts. (2) Pass. You have even distribution. It's a flaw for the dummy to be unable to trump; subtract 1, giving you only 7 points. (3) You have a borderline hand, 8 points. Give yourself a point for good body and bid 4 Hearts. (4) With 9 points, accept. Bid 4 Hearts.

On the same hands, what would you respond if partner made the game-try by bidding 3 Diamonds?

(1) It's 4 Hearts. You have a Heart and a Diamond fit with partner. (2) You have a terrible hand which would normally call for a sign-off, but you want to take aggressive action because your points are in partner's suits. Jump to 4 Hearts. (3) Being able to trump partner's Diamond losers is just what he needs. Say 4 Hearts. (4) You have a strong raise,

but no Diamond help. Bid 3 Hearts. Your Clubs now are of doubtful value.

Let's take another way a trump suit is found early in the bidding. You hold ♠Kxxxx ♡xx ◊QJx ♣Qxx. What is your second bid in each of the following auctions:

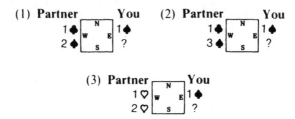

(1) **Partner**   **You**
   1♣   1♠
   2♣   ?

(2) **Partner**   **You**
   1♣   1♠
   3♣   ?

(3) **Partner**   **You**
   1♡   1♠
   2♡   ?

(1) The opener has a minimum, at the most 15 points. Re-valued, your hand is worth 10; you have no interest in game. Pass. (2) Partner has shown additional values, 16-18 points, accept happily. Bid 4 Spades. The combined holding is 26 to 28 points. (3) Partner has a minimum and a six-card Heart suit. Pass. You're in the best spot. At Hearts you have only 8 points.

Although your plan is to take only one bid with 6 to 9, unless partner urges you onward, you might bid a second time if a pass would leave you in a bad contract. When this is the case, be sure the second call is a weak bid.

Partner   **You**
   1♣   1♠
   1 NT   ?

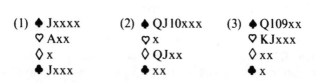

(1) ♠ Jxxxx	(2) ♠ QJ10xxx	(3) ♠ Q109xx
♡ Axx	♡ x	♡ KJxxx
◊ x	◊ QJxx	◊ xx
♣ Jxxx	♣ xx	♣ x

(1) Bid 2 Clubs. Taking partner back to his first-bid suit shows a preference and is not a forward-going bid. (2) Bid 2 Spades to show a long suit and a safer place to play a part-score contract. You would not do this with a stringy suit. (3) Bid 2 Hearts to indicate a two-suited hand unsuitable for No Trump. Partner may pass; a new suit by the responder is not forcing after the opener has rebid 1 No Trump. If this improves partner's hand, he may raise your Hearts. No matter, on this hand don't accept any game invitation.

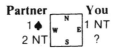

Partner   You
1♠   1 NT
2 NT   ?

Opener has shown a very good hand of 17 or 18 points. He probably had an opening No Trump, but preferred to bid his major. If you're on the lower side of your bid with 6 or 7 points, pass; if you're on the upper side with 8 or 9, accept the invitation and go to 3 No Trump. Here are some examples:

(1) ♠ xx
  ♡ KQxx
  ◊ 109x
  ♣ K10xx

(2) ♠ xx
  ♡ Kxxx
  ◊ Jxx
  ♣ Qxxx

(3) ♠ xx
  ♡ xxx
  ◊ xx
  ♣ AK10xxx

(1) Accept. Your 8 points are good points, two Kings and a Queen, and you have a couple of 10's. (2) Decline. Pass and pray. (3) Your long Clubs look inviting. You may be able to set them up. Take a chance even though you have only 7 points. Go to game.

With 10-12 Points

With an intermediate hand of 10 to 12 points, you have too much for a single raise and not enough for a jump raise.

What you'd really like to do is give a 1-1/2 raise, but you can't do that. Plan to take two forward-going bids, but not insist on a game. Your first bid will have to force partner to bid again so you'll get the opportunity to make the second bid. Therefore, your first response has to be a new suit which is forcing. Then what?

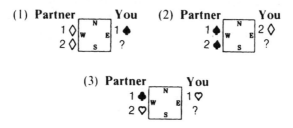

(1) Partner — You
1♢ — 1♠
2♢ — ?

(2) Partner — You
1♠ — 2♢
2♠ — ?

(3) Partner — You
1♣ — 1♡
2♡ — ?

(1) You hold ♠Axxxx ♡QJx ♢xx ♣Axx. There is still a chance for game. A move in that direction is a bid of 2 No Trump.

(2) Your hand is ♠Qxx ♡Jxx ♢AKxxx ♣xx. Now say 3 Spades. You took your two bids; the rest is up to partner.

(3) You have ♠QJx ♡KJxx ♢xx ♣KJ10x. Invite a game with 3 Hearts.

Partner — You
1♢ — 1♠
2♣ — ?

With ♠KQxx ♡Jxx ♢xx ♣AJxx, bid 3 Clubs. Partner asked you to choose between his suits. Tell him you have a Club raise. With a weaker hand, you'd pass and leave him in 2 Clubs. Taking a second bid shows additional values.

With ♠ KQxx ♡ AJ10 ◊ Qxx ♣ xxx, bid 2 No Trump. You have protection in the unbid suits and a semifit with partner.

With 13-15 Points

When you hold 13-15 points opposite a partner who has opened the bidding, you plan to reach a game. An opening hand facing an opening hand will usually produce a game. If your first bid was a jump-raise (Partner - 1 ♡, You - 3 ♡) or a jump in No Trump (Partner - 1 ♡, You - 2 NT), you told your story with one bid. Suppose you named a new suit:

(1) **Partner**   **You**
   1 ♡   1 ♠
   1 NT   ?

(2) **Partner**   **You**
   1 ♡   1 ♠
   2 ◊   ?

(3) **Partner**   **You**
   1 ♡   1 ♠
   4 ♠   ?

(1) You hold ♠ AJxx ♡ xx ◊ KJxx ♣ KJx. This is an easy one; jump to 3 No Trump.

(2) You hold ♠ KQxx ♡ Jx ◊ Axx ♣ Axxx. With an evenly balanced hand, jump to 3 No Trump. You can't raise partner's major; he can't raise yours. The best spot is No Trump.

Holding ♠ Axxx ♡ 10x ◊ KQxx ♣ AJx, you'd have a Diamond fit with partner but 11 tricks are very difficult to get. Jump to 3 No Trump. You have a play for nine tricks. If partner rebids Diamonds, contract for the minor suit game.

Suppose you held ♠ Axxxx ♡ x ◊ Jx ♣ AKJxx. You don't have a fit with either of partner's suits. Go slow; danger ahead. Bid 3 Clubs. If partner rebids Diamonds, showing five-five distribution in the red suits, pass. The first player to suspect a misfit passes. However, if partner raises Spades to show a preference over Clubs, he has three cards in your suit. Go to game in Spades.

(3) You hold ♠KJxx ♡x ◇AJxx ♣KJ10x. Partner's rebid shows 19-21 points. There may be a slam in store for you. Check for Aces via Blackwood.

Partner / You

Partner		You
1◇		1♡
1♠		?

You hold ♠AJ87 ♡K10xxx ◇xx ♣Ax. With your four-card trump support, jump to 3 Spades. When the responder sees game he jumps.

With ♠Axx ♡AJ10xxx ◇Kxx ♣x, jump to 3 Hearts to show a long, strong suit.

With ♠Kxx ♡KQxxx ◇xx ♣KQJ, bid 2 Clubs to suggest five cards in your Heart suit. Partner's next bid will clarify the situation. If he raises Hearts, go to 4 Hearts. If he bids 2 No Trump, bid the No Trump game.

With 16-18 Points

With 16-18 points, you have a big hand. You want to respond in a way to distinguish it from 10-12 or 13-15.

The simplest way to show your points is to jump to 3 No Trump. Although this is a game contract, *it is not a shut-out bid*. Rather, it asks partner to calculate the high-card assets and ascertain the best contract. Of course, you wouldn't bid No Trump if you could raise your partner's major or if you had a major of your own to bid. Here are some examples:

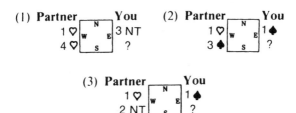

(1) You hold ♠ Kxx ♡ Jx ◊ AKxxx ♣ AQx. Partner's rebid in Hearts shows a six-card trump suit and uneven distribution, unsuitable for No Trump. He has a minimum opener and no interest in slam. Trust him. Pass.

Suppose, after your 3 No Trump, partner bid 4 No Trump. That's an invitation to slam if you're on the top of your bid with 17 or 18. With this hand, you'd happily contract for 6 No Trump.

(2) You hold ♠ KJxxx ♡ Ax ◊ xx ♣ KQxx. Re-evaluated, your hand is worth 16. Added to partner's medium hand of 16-18, there is a slam possibility. As a precautionary measure, use Blackwood to protect against landing in a slam with only two Aces.

(3) You hold ♠ Kxxx ♡ Ax ◊ AKJx ♣ Jxx. This is a classic example of simple arithmetic. At No Trump count only high cards; you have 16 and partner shows 19. Jump right to 6 No Trump. No use to check for Aces. It's impossible for the opponents to have two; there are only 5 points left in the pack.

When you hold 16-18 and a raise for partner's major, you show it by taking three forward-going bids — bid a new suit, then bid another new suit, then give a jump-raise. Partner opened 1 Spade and you hold ♠ AJxx ♡ x ◊ Q10xxx ♣ AKx. The auction might go:

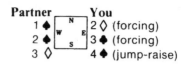

Partner	You
1 ♠	2 ◊ (forcing)
2 ♠	3 ♣ (forcing)
3 ◊	4 ♠ (jump-raise)

With 19 Points or More

With 19 points or more, facing a partner who can open the bidding, concentrate immediately on a slam. If a trump suit has been discovered, initiate Blackwood with 4 No Trump. Even if partner has a bare 13, your 19 gives you 32 points. Landing the slam may depend on a finesse or a lucky lead, but you want to risk it. You want to bid a little slam if you have an even chance to make it. (You bid a grand slam when it's cold.)

When you hold a self-sustaining trump suit of your own, you can flash the slam signal with a jump-shift in a new suit. Since the mere bidding of a new suit forces the opener to speak again, the jump-shift announces the partnership is in the slam zone.

If you need to search further for a contract, prefer to bid your suit merely at the lowest level. When there's exploratory work to be done it's wise to keep the bidding low while you search. A jump-shift crowds the bidding.

Partner opened 1 Spade and you hold:

(1) ♠ Kxxx	(2) ♠ x	(3) ♠ x
♡ KJ10xx	♡ AQJ10xx	♡ AJxx
◊ Axx	◊ KQxx	◊ AQxx
♣ A	♣ Ax	♣ KQJ10

(1) You know you want to play Spades. It's time for Blackwood. Bid 4 No Trump. (2) You don't have a fit with partner but your Hearts are so strong you're willing to attempt a Heart slam even if partner has a singleton.

Jump-shift to 3 Heart. (3) Your hand adds up to 19, counting the Spade singleton, but you don't know where you want to play this one. Keep the bidding low while you explore for a trump suit. Bid only 2 Diamonds. If partner raises Diamonds, or bids Hearts or Clubs, you're ready to GO. If he rebids Spades, fasten your seatbelt, keep a cool head, and bid the Clubs. Make every attempt to play a suit contract.

Drill. VI. Test Your Rebids as Responder

Are You a Good Listener?

Every time your partner bids, he tells you something about his point-count and his distribution. What did he tell you on these?

1. You hold: ♠ J10 ♡854 ◊ AK962 ♣ K102
   The bidding has gone:

Partner		You
1♠		2◊
2♡		2 NT
3♡		?

   (a) How many Spades does partner have?
   (b) How many Hearts does partner have?
   (c) How many points does partner have?
   (d) Is 3 Hearts forcing?
   (e) What would you bid?

2. You hold: ♠ xx ♡ Axxxx ◊ KQJ ♣ xxx
   The bidding has gone:

Partner		You
1♣		1♡
1♠		1 NT
3♡		?

   (a) How many Clubs does partner have?
   (b) How many Spades?
   (c) How many Hearts?
   (d) What's his point-count?
   (e) What do you bid?

3. You hold: ♠ KQxx ♡ xx ◇ Qxxxx ♣ xx
   The bidding has gone:

   Partner   **You**

   (a) How many Hearts does partner have?
   (b) How many points?
   (c) What's your bid?

4. You hold: ♠ J10xx ♡ Qx ◇ AQxx ♣ Kxx
   The bidding has gone:

   Partner   **You**
   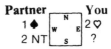

   (a) How many Hearts does partner have?
   (b) How many Spades?
   (c) How many points?
   (d) What's your bid?

5. You are East with ♠ Kx ♡ KJ10xx ◇ xxx ♣ AKx
   The bidding has gone:

   Partner   **You**
   1♠   [N W E S]   2♡
   2 NT   ?

   (a) How many Spades does partner have?
   (b) How many Hearts?
   (c) How many Clubs and Diamonds?
   (d) How many points?
   (e) What's your bid?

21. Finding Two Bids

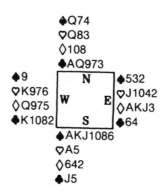

```
              ♠Q74
              ♡Q83
              ◊108
              ♣AQ973
   ♠9          N        ♠532
   ♡K976              ♡J1042
   ◊Q975  W      E    ◊AKJ3
   ♣K1082     S        ♣64
              ♠AKJ1086
              ♡A5
              ◊642
              ♣J5
```

South deals

The bidding:

South	West	North	East
1 Spade	Pass	2 Clubs	Pass
2 Spades	Pass	3 Spades	Pass
4 Spades	All Pass		

When South opened a Spade, North valued his hand at 12 points and planned his two bids. He temporized with 2 Clubs. Now, South rebid his long suit showing a minimum. North encouraged with a raise and South carried on to game. West led the Heart 6.

In a quick analysis of his prospects South saw only eight immediate winners. He decided those Queens were going to have to work. He risked the Heart Queen and it held. Now he played the Spade Ace and King. He abandoned trumps for a moment to see what was working with Clubs.

He played the Club Jack, West covered with the King, forcing the Ace. Now declarer picked up the last Spade, took the winning Club Queen, and conceded three Diamond tricks. He scored his game. He could have made an overtrick if West hadn't covered the Club honor forcing declarer to use two big cards on one trick.

22. Searching for a Trump Suit

By David Flaumenhaft, North Woodmere, N.Y.

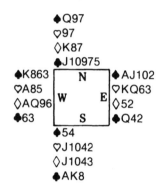

West deals

The bidding:

West	North	East	South
1 Diamond	Pass	1 Heart	Pass
1 Spade	Pass	3 Spades	Pass
4 Spades	All Pass		

East-West sailed smoothly along looking for a trump suit. When the Spade suit was hoisted, East promptly made a limit bid, jumping to show his opening hand. West bid game.

North opened the Club Jack, which held, and continued to partner's Ace-King. Declarer ruffed the third round. West counted eight winners and needed to locate two more. He cashed the trump King, finessed the Jack successfully (creating one winner), and played the Ace to pick up the last outstanding trump.

On the third round of trumps South was squeezed. He had to unguard the Heart Jack or the Diamond Jack. What should he throw? He could *see* Hearts had to be protected, so he discarded the Diamond.

Declarer switched to Hearts to see if he could set up a trick, playing the Ace-King-Queen. But South held the commanding card. Now West had to look in the Diamond suit. He led dummy's deuce, and inserted the 9, a safety play. It forced the King, giving him his game.

A safety play is a precautionary measure taken against a bad break, giving just a little better chance. Declarer realized if North held the Diamond King it would defeat him, so he played the Diamond 9, in case it would force the King. If the 9 had fallen to the Jack or 10, any return North made would give declarer another chance. A Diamond, of course, would come into the Ace-Queen, giving a free finesse. Anything else would be ruffed in dummy, and give declarer another chance to finesse the Diamond Queen. You just can't be too careful at bridge.

23. The New Suit Game-Try

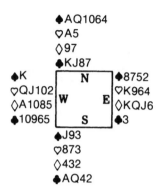

```
              ♠AQ1064
              ♡A5
              ◊97
              ♣KJ87
  ♠K              N        ♠8752
  ♡QJ102                   ♡K964
  ◊A1085   W         E     ◊KQJ6
  ♣10965           S       ♣3
              ♠J93
              ♡873
              ◊432
              ♣AQ42
```

North deals

The bidding:

North	East	South	West
1 Spade	Pass	2 Spades	Pass
3 Clubs	Pass	4 Spades	All Pass

North opened 1 Spade. When South gave a single raise, North's hand re-evaluated at 17, but he wanted to know where his partner's points were; if South didn't have a Club honor he didn't want to be in game. If partner's points were in the red suits, they wouldn't be as helpful. So North bid 3 Clubs, telling partner just that.

North was on track. It was the only kind of game invitation South could accept. South had a terrible hand, couldn't trump a thing, but his points were in the right place. He climbed to 4 Spades.

East led the Diamond King, continued the Queen, and then the Jack, but North stepped out with a Spade. Declarer had to finesse trumps so he went to dummy with the Club

Ace, and played the Spade Jack. The King covered, and North took the Ace. Then he carefully played to the Spade 9, back to the Spade 10, and persisted with his last trump, the Queen, to pick up East's final trump.

Then declarer collected his three Club tricks and Heart Ace, exactly scoring his game.

24. Each Bid Gave a Clue

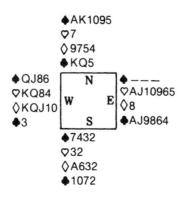

♠AK1095
♥7
♦9754
♣KQ5

♠QJ86
♥KQ84
♦KQJ10
♣3

♠— — —
♥AJ10965
♦8
♣AJ9864

♠7432
♥32
♦A632
♣1072

East deals

The bidding:

East	South	West	North
1 Heart	Pass	1 Spade	Pass
2 Clubs	Pass	2 Diamonds	Pass
3 Clubs	Pass	4 Hearts	Pass
6 Hearts	Pass	Pass	Double
All Pass			

When East opened 1 Heart, West estimated his hand at 17 points and set out to give partner all the clues he could, hoping to reach slam. He bid 1 Spade. North bit his tongue; he'd planned to bid that himself; he had to pass.

On the next go-round, East named his second suit, 2 Clubs, and West mentioned Diamonds. Discouraged, East rebid his Clubs at the lowest level, revealing a minimum hand. Now, West jumped in Hearts. Bidding two new suits and then giving a jump-raise showed 16, 17, or 18, and also indicated a Club void or singleton.

East sat bolt upright. His hand suddenly swelled, high cards = 10, void = 3, singleton = 2, second suit = 1, extra trumps = 3, totalling 19. He bid 6 Hearts like a shot. When the bidding circled around to North he decided he had waited long enough to speak; he was ready with a double.

South cashed the Diamond Ace, and then led a Spade to partner's King, but declarer clobbered it with a trump. East, a man of caution, chose to set up Clubs before using dummy's Hearts to extract trumps. He played the Club Ace, then led his lowest Club and ruffed with the Heart King. He played a low trump to get back to his hand. Again, he played his lowest Club, and ruffed with dummy's Heart Queen. All the Clubs fell. He gathered trumps and tabled his hand, proclaiming every card was a winner.

VII. THE OPENING LEAD

Choosing the opening lead is one of the great challenges of bridge that makes it the fascinating game it is. Whole books have been written about that one card. It has been said if you could always select the correct card, you would win more often than anyone has ever won in bridge. There is judgment on every hand. Even experts will often disagree on a choice.

It's the only play made when you see only 13 cards. After that, the dummy comes down and everyone can see 26 cards. That's why people say the opening lead is made "blind". Sometimes, just as soon as you see dummy, you wish you could take your card back. Even the great Garozzo* sometimes wishes he could take back his card.

You're blind, but you aren't deaf! You heard the bidding, and that furnishes a clue. Form the habit of trying to picture the other hands as the auction progresses. If the opponents did all the bidding, how many points did they show? Add those to yours and estimate how many your partner has. Now, try to imagine where partner's strength is so you can help him get his tricks. Whenever your study reveals that you alone hold all the outstanding face cards, protect them with careful leads.

Your own card combinations may give you a clue. A sequence in honors is always attractive and safe, but you don't get them very often. Lots of time all you can do is guess what to lead, so it helps to be lucky. However, there are a few scientific leads you can learn.

---

*Benito Garozzo, of the famous Italian Blue Team, renowned for his brilliant opening leads.

There are two different lines of strategy. One is employed against No Trump contracts and the other against suit contracts. The way to attack a No Trump contract is more clear cut, so let's analyze that first.

Against No Trump

No Trump declarers, especially those playing 2 No Trump or 3 No Trump, have most of the high cards, lots of Aces and Kings. The 3 No Trump bidder especially is loaded. To defeat him, it's essential to develop tricks out of small cards, so the longer your suit the better your chances. Therefore, you lead your longest suit. The first side that establishes its long suit usually wins the score in a No Trump contract.

Which card do you play? Lead the fourth from the top, or, if you have a sequence headed by an honor, play the top of the sequence:

(1) You lead the 5, partner sacrifices his Queen to the cause, and declarer wins the King. Your suit is established. As soon as you win the lead, you can collect four Spade tricks.

(2) You lead the King, top of a perfect sequence, which pushes out the Ace, and you have four winners. Observe if you led fourth-best you would give declarer a trick with the 10. Don't give presents at the bridge table.

If your suit were <u>K</u>Q1053, you would have an imperfect sequence — the third card is once removed from a perfect sequence. You also lead the top card. When you have an interior sequence headed by an honor, again, you lead the top of the sequence, KJ1094, AQJ92.

When either defender regains the lead, he should continue playing that suit. In returning a suit led by your partner, it is correct to return your best card if you started with three, and to return your original fourth-best if you started with more than three. Holding AJx, you win the Ace and then play back the Jack. Holding AJ72, win the Ace and continue with the deuce.

• When you have two long suits, choose the stronger one. If they are of approximately the same texture, the bidding having given no information about either, prefer a major. Declarer might conceal a long minor, but not a major.

• If your long suit was bid by an opponent, look for another suit. Partner isn't likely to have much help there and you might aid the declarer.

• If your partner bid a suit, it is usually the long suit for your side. It is almost always correct to lead it. Which card do you play? In the examples below, the underscored is correct:

>   —With a doubleton, lead the higher: Jx, Ax, 9x, Kx
>
>   —With three, lead the top of a sequence, low from an honor, top of nothing: QJ10, KQx, Qxx, Axx, 9xx
>
>   —With four or more, top of a sequence, fourth-best from any other holding: KQ109, 9xxx, Kxxxx, KJ109x

Notice when you have an honor in partner's suit and hold three or more cards, you lead a low card. This play has two purposes. It shows partner how many cards you hold, so he can read how many declarer has against him, and keeps your big card behind declarer to kill an important card of his. An example:

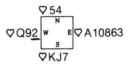

East bid a Heart, but South got to 3 No Trump expecting two Heart winners. West led a low Heart, East won the Ace, and continued the suit. Declarer finessed the Jack but West captured it with the Queen. Obviously if West had led the Queen at trick one, South would have two tricks in the suit.

Against A Suit Contract

The attack against a suit contract is entirely different. Your attention is concentrated on the first two or three rounds of a suit, because soon declarer will be ruffing. Against a No Trump contract, if you held AKQJ10 you would be assured of five tricks, but against a suit contract you would expect only two or three. Against a suit contract the defense must make haste collecting their winners.

The tough decision is choosing the suit to lead. There are only four choices but which one? The one that will bring in tricks the quickest!

• The King from the AKQ is the ideal lead in bridge. You don't get it very often. Or, the King from AKx. Against a suit contract, leading a King promises you also hold the Ace, or the Queen, or both. Leading the Ace and then the King shows a doubleton and a desire to ruff the third round, AK.

• Your partner overcalled. Lead his suit; he might have the AKQ!

• Lead the suit in which you have the most attractive holding: <u>K</u>QJ, <u>K</u>Q10, <u>Q</u>J10.

• An unbid suit. If the opponents bid three suits but failed to land in No Trump the bidding indicates that you and partner hold the fourth suit.

• Lead low from an honor, the higher the honor the better because it will set up quicker: K76<u>2</u>, Q9<u>4</u>, J76<u>2</u>, 1085<u>3</u>. (Exception, not an Ace.)

• Never, never, *never* underlead an Ace in a suit contract at trick one. If you choose to lead a suit in which you hold the Ace, lead the Ace. <u>A</u>72, <u>A</u>Q732. If your partner bid a suit and you have the Ace in it, lead the Ace. Why? The declarer sometimes holds the singleton King, or the declarer may have the King and his dummy a singleton, and you'll never win your Ace. However, after you see the dummy, it is sometimes a good idea to underlead an Ace.

Aces are made to capture Kings and Queens. When you lead an Ace everyone plays little cards. Therefore laying down an Ace is an unattractive lead, unless you have a reason.

• A singleton is a good lead if partner has an entry and can give you a ruff. Consequently, it is a better lead from a weak hand than from a strong hand.

The opponents are in 4 Spades and you're on opening lead holding:

(1)	♠A72	(2)	♠752	(3)	♠QJ3
	♡6		♡6		♡7
	◇A864		◇9852		◇K7652
	♣A9642		♣109642		♣J863

With (1) don't lead your singleton. Your partner doesn't have any entries; you have all of them. Play the Club Ace. With (2) the singleton is a good lead; your partner has the entries. A Heart ruff is your only chance to help set the contract. With (3) the singleton is undesirable because you have a natural trump trick and no trumps to spare ruffing. Prefer a small Diamond. If you had a surplus trump, like Kxx, the singleton would be preferred.

• A doubleton, hoping for a third-round ruff. Sometimes employed to avoid other embarrassing leads. Ax, Jx, 9x.

* * **Scientific Leads** * *

• When you have declarer's second suit and the bidding indicates dummy has few or no cards in it, lead a trump to cut down on dummy's ruffing power. The bidding has gone:

South	North
1 Spade	1 No Trump
2 Hearts	3 Hearts
4 Hearts	

You hold ♠KJ972 ♡96 ♢K74 ♣Q42. Lead the trump 9. When you win the lead again, play another trump. If partner obtains the lead he should follow your strategy. You're trying to prevent declarer from trumping your Spade winners in dummy. A declarer leans heavily on dummy's ruffing value.

You don't lead a trump because you're in doubt. You lead a trump to stop a crossruff.

• When you have lots of trumps, four or more, lead your longest suit, even from an awkward holding. You hope declarer will be short in it and ruff. You hope to cut down declarer's trumps until you have more than he has. The strategy is to try to gain control of the hand.

* * **Lead Indicating Doubles** * *

• Sometimes you will get a golden opportunity to tell your partner specifically which suit to open. Any double of

.an artificial bid is lead directing. A response to Blackwood is a case:

South	West	North	East
1 Spade	Pass	3 Spades	Pass
4 NT	Pass	5 Diamonds	Double
6 Spades	All Pass		

East's double of the artificial 5 Diamond bid shows an attractive Diamond holding and asks West to lead the suit.

• A double of a No Trump contract also calls for the lead of a specific suit — the defenders' suit if either bid; otherwise, dummy's first-bid suit.

South	West	North	East
1 Spade	Pass	2 NT	Pass
3 NT	Double	All Pass	

West's double asks partner to lead dummy's suit, Spades, and if he does, West believes the contract is doomed.

However, suppose over the Spade bid, West overcalled Clubs, and North-South wound up in 3 No Trump. Then, West doubled. He is asking for the lead of his suit, Clubs. "Don't let them scare you out of leading my suit, partner. If you lead it, I can set them."

• The double of a slam contract is always lead-directing. Known as the Lightner Slam Double after its inventor it demands an unusual lead. The theory is a slam bidder seldom goes down more than one. Who cares about the few points the double brings? The urgent matter is to set the contract. Therefore, the double of a slam is reserved as a lead-director. It says, "Partner, do not make a normal lead. I have a surprise holding in a suit you would not normally lead."

The double says, "Don't lead my suit, don't lead your suit, don't lead an unbid suit." Lead the most unusual suit you can imagine—the first side-suit bid by dummy or by declarer. It is never trumps.

South	West	North	East
1 ♠	3 ◊	Pass	6 ◊
Double			

If South hadn't doubled, North would be expected to lead partner's suit, a Spade, but the double distinctly warns, "Don't lead a Spade! Lead a Club or a Heart." South is probably void in one and North should be able to tell which one by looking at his own distribution.

The Rule Of Eleven

The Rule of Eleven is an infallible mathematical formula that card players have been using profitably for 200 years. It operates when the opening lead is the fourth-best card in a suit — the card most often led in bridge. The formula enables the third player and the declarer to deduce immediately how many cards each other player holds higher than the card led.

It looks like magic, but it's simple arithmetic. This is how it works. Suppose you wanted to know how many cards in the spade suit were higher than the Spade 6. You would subtract 6 from 14. (After the 10, the Jack is 11, the Queen 12, the King 13, and the Ace 14.) You learn there are 8 cards higher.

Now, if your partner led the 6 spot and it was his fourth-best card, he kept in his hand three cards higher. Allowing for those three, you subtract the 6 from 11 — not 14 — and the remainder is the number of cards higher than the 6 spot in the other three hands.

Since the third player can see how many he holds and how many dummy holds, he can tell how many the declarer has. Similarly, the declarer sees his own and dummy's, so he can deduce how many the third player has. This example illustrates it:

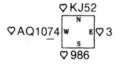

West leads the Heart 7. Now East does his arithmetic: 11 - 7 = 4. There are four cards higher than the 7 in the North, East, and South hands. Since East can see two of them in his hand and two of them in dummy he knows declarer doesn't have any. If dummy's 3 is played, East can play low, confident partner's 7 will win. If dummy's 9 is played, East covers with the Jack, confident it will hold the trick, reserving the Ace to smother the King.

Another deal shows a case when the formula benefits declarer:

West leads the Heart 7. Declarer subtracts 7 from 11 = 4. Seeing all the four outstanding Hearts that can top the 7 are in his own hand and dummy's, he plays dummy's deuce, knowing the 8 in his own hand will win the trick. The rule often enables a player to make such a frugal play.

VII. Test Your Opening Leads

Assume you're on opening lead with each of the following hands. First, choose the lead you'd make against 3 No Trump. Then, choose your lead against 3 Clubs. (No adverse bidding.)

	Against 3NT	Against 3 Clubs
1. ♠A8532 ♡963 ◇QJ104 ♣9	_____	_____
2. ♠Q32 ♡KJ1094 ◇763 ♣92	_____	_____
3. ♠A5 ♡J974 ◇J974 ♣753	_____	_____
4. ♠AJ1094 ♡8 ◇75 ♣KJ1096	_____	_____
5. ♠AQ105 ♡QJ105 ◇85 ♣975	_____	_____
6. ♠AK972 ♡972 ◇98 ♣973	_____	_____
7. ♠AK62 ♡QJ109 ◇1032 ♣74	_____	_____
8. ♠1092 ♡92 ◇1092 ♣98532	_____	_____

Your partner overcalled Diamonds but the opponents wound up in 4 Hearts. What's your lead with:

9. ♠J1094 ♡763 ◇K4 ♣KJ42
10. ♠9 ♡A72 ◇9753 ♣J5432
11. ♠8 ♡K10652 ◇9753 ♣972

The bidding went:

North	South
1 Spade	2 Clubs
2 Hearts	3 Hearts
4 Hearts	

What's your opening lead from:

12. ♠KJ52 ♡93 ◇86 ♣A9752

Choose your opening lead after this auction:

You	North	East	South
1 Spade	Pass	Pass	1 No Trump
Pass	3 No Trump	Double	Pass

13. ♠AJ954 ♡KQ107 ◇A4 ♣92

25. Choosing a Lead Against No Trump

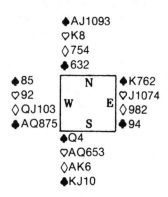

South deals

The bidding:

South	West	North	East
1 Heart	Pass	1 Spade	Pass
2 NT	Pass	3 NT	All Pass

South's rebid of 2 No Trump, jumping the bidding one level, showed 19 points and North carried on to game. West led his longest suit, Clubs, and chose his fourth-best, the 7. Declarer won the 10.

South saw it was important to keep East out of the lead to avoid a play through his Club holding. With a choice of two good suits, he first tried the Hearts, playing low to the King, back to the Queen, and then laying down the Ace. The suit failed to split and East, the dangerous opponent, held the top Heart.

Now South had to risk the Spade finesse. He led the Queen and let it ride but East came out with the King. He returned his last Club, declarer played the Jack, and West won the Queen. Now West played the Club Ace, bringing in all the outstanding Clubs. He collected the Club 8 and 5, putting declarer down one.

Next, West led the Diamond Queen but South won the King, took the Diamond Ace and then played over to the high Spades, winning the rest.

26. A Scientific Lead

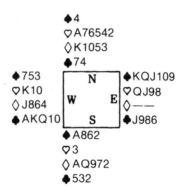

```
              ♠4
              ♡A76542
              ◊K1053
              ♣74
♠753        ┌─────────┐    ♠KQJ109
♡K10        │    N    │    ♡QJ98
◊J864       │ W     E │    ◊——
♣AKQ10      │    S    │    ♣J986
            └─────────┘
              ♠A862
              ♡3
              ◊AQ972
              ♣532
```

West deals

All vulnerable

The bidding:

West	North	East	South
1 Club	Pass	1 Spade	Pass
1 NT	Pass	3 Hearts	Pass
3 Spades	Pass	4 Spades	All Pass

Bridge players love to lead singletons. It's like getting something for nothing to win a trick with a tiny trump. So South led the Heart 3. He was lucky (he thought) to find his partner with the Ace and able to give him an immediate ruff.

Since he held the top trump, South foresaw he could sink the contract with his Diamond Ace, so he laid it on the table. Declarer speared it with a trump and played the trump King. South won his Ace, switched back to Diamonds, and declarer ruffed again.

East completed the gathering of trumps. It took every Spade he had, but he was home. He held two reigning Hearts and four top Clubs, bringing his total up to 10. The score was +620 for East-West. It was duplicate — the vulnerable game counted 500 plus the trick score of 120.

The duplicate board moved to the next table where the bidding was identical. Here sat a South who had heard the bridge bromide, "When you are long in trumps, lead your longest suit." This South began his fight with the Diamond Ace (an awkward holding to lead from, but he trusted the b.b.).

Declarer ruffed with the Spade 9 and continued with the trump King. South topped it with the Ace and returned another Diamond to force the strong hand to trump again. Declarer ruffed with the Spade 10. Then he played the Spade Queen. South followed but North discarded a Heart. East blinked, counted again. Oh, no! Ohhh, yes! South held two trumps, declarer only one.

East played to the Heart King, but North won the Ace and continued partner's strategy with a third Diamond lead, the King. Declarer ruffed with his last trump. He collected three Club tricks and then tried the Heart Queen, but South trumped with the Spade 6. Then South led the Spade 8 to pick up the last outstanding trump, dummy's Spade 7. Now South rolled out his last two Diamonds while declarer helplessly discarded high Hearts.

East won four Spade tricks — three of them ruffing Diamonds — three Club tricks, and no Hearts. Down three! The score went in the other column: North-South +300.

Our second East never played a single wrong card. He couldn't survive against the destructive defense fired at him from both sides.

27. Lead-Indicating Double

By Carole Amster, of Fairfax, Va.

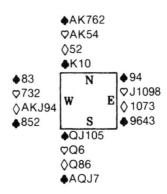

♠AK762
♡AK54
◇52
♣K10

♠83　　　♠94
♡732　　　♡J1098
◇AKJ94　　◇1073
♣852　　　♣9643

♠QJ105
♡Q6
◇Q86
♣AQJ7

North deals

The bidding:

North	East	South	West
1 Spade	Pass	3 Spades	Pass
4 NT	Pass	5 Diamonds	Double
5 Spades	All Pass		

When South offered a jump-raise, North re-evaluated his hand at 20 points, and believed he had a slam. He checked for Aces with Blackwood, and South bid 5 Diamonds to show one.

Now West entered the picture with a double. It was a lead-indicating double telling partner exactly which suit to play at trick one.

East got the message. As the bidding progressed he had been studying his cards and had decided to open his Heart Jack, the top of his sequence. Partner's double vetoed that.

North got the message, too. Staring at two worthless Diamonds, he signed off at 5 Spades.

East led the Diamond 3, West won the Jack and took his King. When he laid down the Ace declarer trumped with the Spade Ace. He pulled trumps and took all the rest of the tricks, making 5 Spades.

If West had been nodding, neglecting to take advantage of his opportunity to tell partner what to lead, North would have contracted for 6 Spades. With the Jack of Hearts lead, declarer would gallop off with 13 tricks! Six Spades (one being a Heart ruff in dummy), four Clubs (pitching losing Diamonds from his hand), and three Hearts — earning a slam bonus.

128

28. The Revealing Rule of Eleven

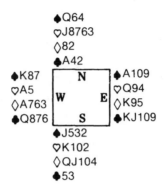

```
              ♠Q64
              ♡J8763
              ◊82
              ♣A42
♠K87      ┌─────────┐   ♠A109
♡A5       │    N    │   ♡Q94
◊A763     │ W     E │   ◊K95
♣Q876     │    S    │   ♣KJ109
          └─────────┘
              ♠J532
              ♡K102
              ◊QJ104
              ♣53
```

East deals

The bidding:

East	South	West	North
1 Club	Pass	2 NT	Pass
3 NT	All Pass		

After East opened a Club, West jumped to 2 No Trump, showing an opening hand and denying interest in a major. East carried on to game. North led fourth-best of his longest suit, the Heart 6.

Declarer paused to plan. He counted eight winners — two Spades, three Clubs, two Diamonds, and one Heart. For the ninth his only possible source was one of dummy's Hearts.

Declarer was a faithful follower of the Rule of Eleven, so he carefully did his arithmetic, 11 - 6 = 5, and learned there were five cards higher than the 6 in the East, South, and West hands. Declarer could see two of them in dummy and one in his hand, so he knew South had two higher cards. He played a low Heart from dummy to see what would happen.

South, too, had been doing his mathematics and deduced declarer held only one card higher than the 6. On the bidding he believed this card to be the Ace, so he played the 2! As a result of this amazing play, declarer went down.

West won the Heart Ace and went after Clubs. When North won the Club Ace, he played another Heart. Declarer decided it was time to risk the Heart Queen, but South covered with the King, and continued the Heart 10 which North overtook with his Jack. Then North cashed two more Hearts. The contract was down one.

At trick one, if South had wasted his King, declarer would have a winner in the Queen for his ninth trick. If South had played the 10, declarer could later lead a Heart to dummy's 9 to develop a trick.

- - - -

What about the principle of third hand playing high? Didn't that apply to South? That principle is almost absolute, but not quite. The exception comes when dummy holds important high cards which South must stand guard over to keep them from becoming winners. How does South know? By using the Rule of Eleven!

VIII. DEFENSIVE BIDDING

Half the hands you get at bridge will be opened by your opponents before you have a chance to bid. People have long assumed the player who **opens** the bidding holds an advantage. The reason is most players know all the opening bids and responses, but are unsure of defensive bids and are fuzzy on responses.

Let's unravel that Gordian knot, because defensive bids can be just as descriptive as opening bids.

You have four possible categories of defensive bids from which to choose to describe different hand patterns and different point-count strength. Some of them are even more descriptive than those available to the opener! When you understand the differences in these bidding weapons you will be able to compete just as ably in second position as you can in first.

1. **The overcall,** bidding a suit or No Trump at the lowest level after the opponents have opened the bidding.

2. **The preemptive jump overcall,** jumping the bidding one level or more (dealer - 1 ♦, you - 3 ♦) to crowd the bidding and to show a long suit. If the opponent had passed, you would have opened with a preemptive bid.

3. **The take-out double,** (a) doubling the opponent's bid to get partner to name his best suit, or (b) showing a hand too strong for a simple overcall.

4. **The cue bid,** calling the same suit the opponent bid, directly over him (dealer - 1 ♦, you - 2 ♦) a gigantic take-out double, forcing to game. If the opponent had passed you would have opened with a strong two bid.

* * The Overcall * *

An overcall at the 1-level guarantees a good five-card suit and a minimum of one and a half quick tricks.* These requirements increase with the level of the overcall and the status of the vulnerability because of the danger the next player might double for penalties.

When your opponent opens the bidding, you exercise care coming into the auction because your partner, who has not been heard from, might have an empty hand. You might find yourself alone in the world with no high cards but your own to win tricks. Therefore, when you overcall, you need the security of a good trump suit.

Suit Strength

A great majority of overcalling is at the 1-level. The suit should be strong enough so you won't lose more than two tricks in it if it becomes the trump suit. Ideally, you hold two of the three top honors. Secondary cards are important — 10's, 9's, 8's. These "body" cards reduce the probability of a double. If you hold them, the opponent doesn't, and if he doesn't he isn't likely to double you. A minimum holding for an overcall at the 1-level might be KQ98x or AJ109x.

The foremost object of overcalling is to tell your partner what to lead. This is another reason you need top cards. You might open the bidding with a scroungy suit like J9763, but don't overcall with it.

When you have a two-suited hand, you can overcall with a weaker suit because you have another suit to run to. If

---

*A quick trick is a high card that is expected to win a trick in the first or second round of a suit: AK of same suit = 2, AQ of same suit = 1½, A = 1, KQ of the same suit = 1, Kx = ½.

partner doesn't have support for the first suit, the odds are he has support for the other suit. With two suits of equal length overcall with the higher-ranking first. With ♠9 ♡87 ◊QJ642 ♣AKJ87 overcall 2 Diamonds. If partner doesn't react favorably, next time around bid Clubs.

Be wary of overcalling with length in the enemy's suit because that increases the chance his partner won't be able to raise him, and might like to double you. A pass is sometimes a good bid even with a good hand.

Therefore, the $64 question is: Are you vulnerable and at what level do you have to bid? Suppose North opens 1 Heart. You're East; when do you overcall?

The 1-level overcall *non-vulnerable* shows 10* to 15 points. Notice the upper limit; it's important. Your hand is ♠KQ984 ♡xx ◊xxx ♣AJx. You have 10 high-card points and a good five-card suit, overcall 1 Spade.

The 1-level overcall *vulnerable* shows an opening hand, 13-15. You want to be stronger vulnerable because the penalty will be greater if you run into a bad lay of the cards. With ♠AJ109x ♡xx ◊KQx ♣Kxx you have 13 high-card points and a good suit. Overcall 1 Spade.

The 2-level overcall warrants an opening hand and a good six-card suit or a very strong five-card suit. There are many hands that rate a 1-level overcall but not a 2-level overcall. You have more to lose so you want to have a reasonable play for six tricks. With ♠Ax ♡xx ◊KQJxxx ♣Qxx overcall 2 Diamonds. You have a good suit, an opening hand, and a reasonable chance to turn six tricks.

The 3-level overcall (dealer - 3 ♡, you - 3 ♠) requires 16 points and a good six-card suit. With ♠AKJ109x ♡x ◊AKJx ♣xx overcall a preemptive 3 Hearts with 3 Spades.

_____

*Duplicate bridge has become so aggressive many players overcall non-vulnerable with as few as 8 points.

You have a reasonable play for eight tricks in your own hand.

It is strategically important to overcall every chance you get if you're to be a winning player. An overcall tells your partner what to lead. It sets the stage for a possible game, a part-score, or a sacrifice. Frequently it jams the bidding and creates a problem for the opponents. When an opponent opens 1 Club and you overcall 1 Spade, you rob them of their up-the-line bidding, making it difficult for them to find the Heart suit. Over 1 Diamond an overcall of 2 Clubs is an obstruction, too.

In Fourth Seat

When an opponent bids and his partner passes, you can take greater liberties. It is likely your partner has some strength and you may compete with very little.

South	West	North	East
1♡	Pass	Pass	?

(1) ♠ K10xxx	(2) ♠ Kxx	(3) ♠ xxx
♡ xx	♡ xx	♡ AQ9xx
◊ QJx	◊ AQ9xx	◊ Ax
♣ Kxx	♣ Qxx	♣ Kxx

(1) Compete with 1 Spade. If you pass, the auction will end. When you bid in the "pass-out" seat, you don't promise full values. You just don't wish to sell out cheap. If partner perks up and gives you a raise — even a jump-raise — you can pass. A partner who has passed cannot force. (His jump shows 11 or 12, just under an opening.)

(2) Bid 2 Diamonds, although you don't have full requirements.

(3) Pass. Let the opponents play in your favorite suit.

Responding to Overcalls

Let's move around the table and see how to respond to an overcall. The most encouraging bid is to raise. Let that be your first thought and your second thought.

• You can give **a single raise** with three-card support and 6 to 10 points. It helps your partner to learn he has uncovered a trump suit. It might alert him to a possible sacrifice, and it will help him on the defense.

Don't be timid! If you fail to raise when you can, you will find your partner overbidding to compensate.

• A **jump-raise from 1 to 3** shows at least three trumps and 11 to 13 points (count your hand like dummy points). This bid gives you the best of two worlds — it's a preemptive tactic if partner made a weak overcall, and a game-try if partner overcalled with a good hand.

South	Partner	North	You
1♣	1♠	Pass	?

Holding ♠Qxx ♡AKJxx ◊xxx ♣xx, jump to 3 Spades; don't bid Hearts. Partner doesn't need to know where your points are; he just needs to know you have them.

A jump-raise to game in partner's suit describes a hand long in trumps, weak in high cards, and highly distributional. (It's just like the weak-freak when partner opens one of a major and you jump to 4.) Partner overcalls 1 Spade and you hold ♠Kxxxx ♡x ◊Axxxx ♣xx. Jump to game.

With a big hand of 13 points or more, cue-bid the opponent's suit and later give a single raise. This gives your partner an opportunity to stop if he made a weak overcall. You hold ♠Axxx ♡xx ◊KQJ ♣QJxx, and the bidding has gone:

South	Partner	North	You
1♡	1♠	Pass	2♡ (Cue-bid)
Pass	2♠	Pass	?

A bid of 3 Spades is enough. Your cue-bid told partner you wanted to play game in his suit. He declined with a minimum rebid. A single raise is a second invitation. Give partner an out if he doesn't want to come to the party. You have defined your hand; let partner, the person with the undefined hand, make the decision.

When You Can't Raise

When you can't raise partner's overcall, but you have a fair hand, consider bidding No Trump. This shows a balanced hand and at least one sure trick in the opponent's suit. Bid:

> 1 No Trump with 8 to 10
> 2 No Trump with 11 to 12

If you have a suit of your own and want to interject it into the auction, be aware it is a discouraging bid, shows a lack of trump support for partner, and is not forcing. You wouldn't bid your suit just because you thought it might be prettier than partner's.

South	Partner	North	You
1♢	1♠	Pass	?

Holding ♠ xx ♡ AKJ10xx ♢ xx ♣ xxx, bid 2 Hearts. This shows a good six-card suit.

When you have a horrible holding in partner's suit, a singleton or a void, it's generally dangerous to try to rescue. You usually get in deeper. Partner might have a singleton or a void in your suit! If he gets whacked with a penalty double, then it's time to consider risking a bid of your own long suit. Now, he'll know there's danger ahead, and you're trying to bail him out. It will warn him not to bid again.

No Trump Overcalls

The requirement for overcalling 1 No Trump is exactly the same as an opening 1 No Trump except you need a sure trick in the opponent's suit, preferably two. Responses are the same also.

South	Partner	North	You
1 ♡	1 NT	Pass	?

With ♠ Kxx ♡ xx ◊ AJxx ♣ xxxx bid 2 No Trump; you have eight points. Add a Queen anywhere and you can bid 3 No Trump. The responder need not worry about protection in the adversaries' suit; the overcaller has that.

Tip

You respond to a 2-level overcall with the same count as responding to a 1-level overcall. It's partner's hand that's stronger. In a pinch you can raise a 2-level overcall with only two trumps, since this overcall is usually a six-card suit.

* * The Preemptive Jump Overcall * *

The jump overcall — jumping the bidding one or more levels — is a preemptive bid made on a weak hand with a long suit, not more than 9 or 10 high-card points and most of that in the trump suit. The preemptive overcaller uses the Rule of Two or Three to select the level of the overcall. That is, you count your tricks and overbid your hand three tricks if you're not vulnerable and two tricks if vulnerable.

The purpose is to deprive the enemy of bidding space and make them bid at such a high level they have to guess and, hopefully, will guess wrong.

This bid denies the strength of an opening bid. If an opponent had not opened the bidding you would have made a preemptive bid of 3 or 4 or 5 in a suit. As a preemptive overcaller you have an extra arrow in your quiver. You can also make a preemptive bid at the 2-level. (Dealer - 1♣, You - 2♠). Originally this single jump overcall was a strong bid, but the opportunity to use it arose so seldom, virtually all experts abandoned it for the weak jump overcall.

Here are some examples after an opponent opened 1 Club:

(1)	♠ KJ10xxx	(2)	♠ x	(3)	♠ AQ10xxxx
	♡ x		♡ KQJxxxx		♡ Kx
	◊ Qxx		◊ xx		◊ Kx
	♣ xxx		♣ Kxx		♣ xx

(1) With Spades as trumps you might take five tricks. Not vulnerable, overcall 2 Spades. Vulnerable, pass.

(2) If Hearts are trumps you hope to win seven tricks. Not vulnerable, bid 4 Hearts. Vulnerable, 3 Hearts is enough.

(3) Overcall 1 Spade. You're too strong for a weak jump overcall, and you have lots of strength outside your long suit.

Responding to a Weak Jump Overcall

Let's pretend your partner just made a weak jump overcall. How do you respond? It's just like responding to a preemptive bid; count your quick tricks, add them to partner's tricks, and bid game if you have enough and pass if you don't. Only quick tricks are useful, because the preempter's side suits are usually short enough to ruff the third round.

You need very little trump support. The higher the level of the jump overcall the more trumps partner has. At the 2-level, he usually has six cards, so you'd need two-card support; at the 3-level, usually seven cards, so a singleton is enough.

With a bad hand and three or four cards in partner's suit, you might wish to further the preempt for a sacrifice.

North	Partner	South	You
1♡	2♠	3◇	?

Holding ♠xxxx ♡xx ◇Kx ♣Jxxxx, bid 4 Spades. You have little hope partner will make it but you can see the opponents have a Heart game. Partner doesn't have much and neither do you. You hope at this high level they'll guess wrong, passing when they could make 5 Hearts, or bidding 6 Hearts when they can only make 5 Hearts.

Tip

The weak jump overcall is made over the opening bid of a suit, not over No Trump.

VIII. Test Your Defensive Overcalls

Over an opening 1 Spade what would you bid, non-vulnerable, with:

(1) ♠ xx
♡ AKQ98
◊ Axx
♣ Jxx

(2) ♠ xx
♡ Kxx
◊ AQxxx
♣ Qxx

(3) ♠ AJ10xx
♡ x
◊ AQxx
♣ Kxx

(4) ♠ x
♡ AQJ10942
◊ xx
♣ Jxx

(5) ♠ x
♡ xx
◊ K10xxx
♣ AQJ10x

(6) ♠ QJ10x
♡ xx
◊ AK752
♣ Kx

The auction has gone

South	West	North	East
1♠	1♡	2♠	?

What would you bid with:

(7) ♠ 10xxx
♡ Qxx
◊ Axxx
♣ xx

(8) ♠ Kxxxx
♡ xx
◊ Kxx
♣ Kxx

(9) ♠ AJ109x
♡ xxx
◊ Axx
♣ xx

(10) ♠ AQJ98x
♡ xx
◊ Qxx
♣ xx

(11) ♠ K109x
♡ Jx
◊ J10xx
♣ AQx

(12) ♠ A9xxx
♡ ---
◊ Q762
♣ Kxxx

(13) ♠ x
♡ Qxxxx
◊ Axxxx
♣ xx

(14) ♠ A10xx
♡ xx
◊ QJ10x
♣ AJ9

29. Overcalling to Direct a Lead

By Becky Levering

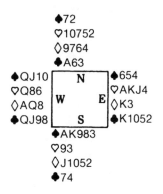

South deals

The bidding:

South	West	North	East
Pass	1 Club	Pass	1 Heart
1 Spade	1 NT	Pass	3 NT
All Pass			

South overcalled a Spade to alert his partner to a favorable lead. West had the suit protected, and bid No Trump. With 14 points, East carried on to game. North led the Spade 7, the top of his doubleton.

What card should South play? South realized he had to give up one round of Spades to set up the suit. With no outside entry, South decided it was time for the ducking play, hoping partner had one more Spade and one more entry. He held back his big cards, but signaled with the Spade 8 that he desired a continuation of the suit. West won the 10, but his contract was doomed.

When declarer led a Club, North seized his Ace and laid down his last Spade. Now, South was ready to play his big cards. He stepped out with the King, next the Ace, and then collected two more Spades, setting the contract one trick.

South was a hero twice. If he had neglected to overcall, partner probably would lead a Diamond, and declarer could rake in 10 tricks, because he could establish his long suit before the opponents could establish their long suit. In addition, if South had erred and won the first round of Spades, declarer again could walk away with his game. South's hold up was just as vital as his bid.

30. Painting West Into a Corner

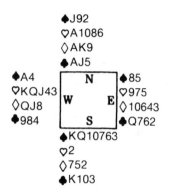

```
              ♠J92
              ♡A1086
              ◊AK9
              ♣AJ5
   ♠A4         ┌─────────┐    ♠85
   ♡KQJ43      │    N    │    ♡975
   ◊QJ8        │ W     E │    ◊10643
   ♣984        │    S    │    ♣Q762
              └─────────┘
              ♠KQ10763
              ♡2
              ◊752
              ♣K103
```

West deals

The bidding:

West	North	East	South
1 Heart	1 NT	Pass	4 Spades
All Pass			

When North overcalled a No Trump, South knew his partnership had a trump suit. Counting his long trumps, South evaluated his assets at 13, and bid the Spade game. West led the Heart King.

Declarer won dummy's Heart Ace and led a low trump to his King. West took his trump Ace, and continued the Heart Queen, but declarer ruffed. Then, South led a low trump to dummy's Jack drawing all the outstanding trumps. He led a Heart and ruffed in his hand. He played to the Diamond Ace, and led dummy's last Heart, again trumping in his own hand. He took the Diamond King.

South had a two-way finesse against the Club Queen and was uncertain which way to take it. If he had to guess, he would say West the Bidder had it. But, South knew a way to remove the guesswork. He was going to get an opponent to lead Clubs for him! How?

By stripping his hand and dummy of Hearts and Diamonds, South had just set the stage for an end play. Here was the situation:

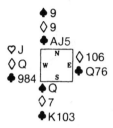

Now, South led a Diamond. It didn't matter which opponent won it, because neither had a palatable play. Any lead would present declarer a trick — a Club would eliminate declarer's guess on the Queen, and a red card would permit him to trump in one hand as he discarded a Club in the other.

West, of course, won the Diamond trick, and led the Club 9. Declarer let it ride to his hand. East came out with the Queen, and South topped it with the King. Now dummy's Ace-Jack were commanding Clubs. South's astute play guaranteed him an overtrick, and he got a smile from his partner to boot.

31. The Bidding Tells a Tale

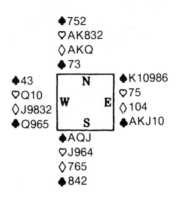

```
              ♠752
              ♡AK832
              ◊AKQ
              ♣73
    ♠43          N        ♠K10986
    ♡Q10                  ♡75
    ◊J9832   W       E    ◊104
    ♣Q965        S        ♣AKJ10
              ♠AQJ
              ♡J964
              ◊765
              ♣842
```

North deals

The bidding:

North	East	South	West
1 Heart	1 Spade	2 Hearts	Pass
3 Hearts	Pass	4 Hearts	All Pass

After North made a game-try with a bid of 3 Hearts, South re-evaluated his Spades. The bidding indicated they were all winners so he valued them as AKQ. After subtracting for even distribution, he had 10, and could well afford to accept the invitation.

East led the Club King and West signaled come-on with the Club 9. East cashed the Ace and West completed the signal with the Club 5. East continued with the Club Jack, but declarer ruffed.

North played the Ace-King of Hearts bringing in all the opponents trumps. Then he led a low Spade and finessed the Jack which won. He came back to his hand with a Diamond to play another Spade and successfully finesse the Queen. He cashed the Spade Ace and claimed, making an overtrick.

The innocent Spade overcall gave South the courage to contract for game. Nevertheless, East should overcall. If West's and South's Spades were exchanged, the overcall would lead East-West to a 3 Spade contract.

32. Making the Opponents Guess

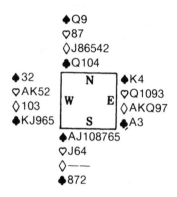

```
                    ♠Q9
                    ♡87
                    ◊J86542
                    ♣Q104
        ♠32          ┌─────────┐      ♠K4
        ♡AK52        │    N    │      ♡Q1093
        ◊103         │ W     E │      ◊AKQ97
        ♣KJ965       │    S    │      ♣A3
                     └─────────┘
                    ♠AJ108765
                    ♡J64
                    ◊——
                    ♣872
```

East deals

East-West vulnerable

The bidding:

East	South	West	North
1 Diamond	3 Spades	4 Clubs	4 Spades
6 Diamonds	All Pass		

The American Contract Bridge League sponsors four charity games a year, almost doubling the usual master point awards to lure bridge players to help the Arthritis Foundation.

Identical hands are played simultaneously in thousands of cities. After the game, players receive a printed record of each hand with an expert analysis of the best bidding and play. It's a lot of fun to study this instant replay.

Here's a hand from the 1977 Spring charity event where a preemptive overcall precipitated amazing bidding at a table of all life masters.

After East opened a Diamond, South jumped to 3 Spades to jam the bidding. West stepped in with his longest suit, bidding 4 Clubs. With a poor hand, North sensed the opponents held a slam and threw another monkey wrench in the bidding machinery with 4 Spades.

East pushed the throttle wide open and bid 6 Diamonds. Everybody passed.

South led his Spade Ace and continued the suit to declarer's King. Crossing to the Heart King, declarer pulled out the trump 10. North followed low and declarer did too. The 10 won, but declarer winced when he saw South play a black card.

The sad story was soon ended but the pain lingered on. Able to turn only 11 tricks, East had to concede a trump trick to North.

"Partner," said South, pointing a finger of scorn, "you had six trumps and you couldn't find a double?"

"No," said North, entering his +200 score. "Your preempt was a vital clue. It told me you didn't have anything in the Heart suit. Neither did I. I was the first to know East should be playing 6 Hearts. I wasn't going to warn him with a double. It was time to play possum."

The biggest swings in score at bridge are said to be caused by preemptive bids. Here lies one more.

IX. OTHER DEFENSIVE BIDS

* * THE TAKE-OUT DOUBLE * *

The double was originally designed to penalize the opponents when they bid too much and its full name was the penalty double. In the early 1900's, a bridge genius came along and created an imaginative second use for the bid. Since a penalty double generally was used only at a high level, a double at a low level could be used to ask partner to name his best suit. Thus, the take-out double was born.

The take-out double means just what the name implies, "Partner, take me out of this double; you can do so by bidding your best suit."

It is easy to distinguish a take-out double. The double of an opponent's suit, which is bid below game-level, is a take-out double if partner has not bid, and if it is made at the first opportunity. It is one of the most useful bids in bridge and adds immense zest to the game.

West	North	East	South
Pass	1♡	Double	Pass
?			

This is a take-out double because West has not made a bid, and West is expected to name his best suit.

West	North	East	South
1♠	2♡	Double	Pass
?			

This is a penalty double because West has made a bid, and West is expected to pass.

There are two kinds of take-out doubles. One is to ask partner to name a trump suit. The other is to show a hand that very well may have a trump suit, but is too strong for a simple overcall.

1. Asking for Partner's Best Suit

In its most classic form, the take-out double describes an opening hand with support for each of the unbid suits, and shortness in the suit opened. Over 1 Heart, a take-out double says, "Partner, please bid 1 Spade, or 2 Clubs, or 2 Diamonds, whichever you prefer. In each case, my hand will be an attractive dummy."

The ideal hand pattern for a take-out double is to have no cards in the opener's suit and be 4-4-5 in the other suits. Holding ♠ AJxx ♡ -- ◇ Axxx ♣ AJ10xx, a player wouldn't overcall Clubs and risk missing a Spade fit with partner. He'd double. The next best hand pattern is to have a singleton in the opener's suit and be 4-4-4 in the others. With either, it is enough to hold 12 high-card points, ♠ KQxx ♡x ◇ K10xx ♣ Axxx. Lacking this perfect distribution, you compensate with additional strength.

A take-out double puts strong emphasis on support for an unbid major suit. The double of one major promises four cards in the other major. The double of a minor shows four cards in each major. It is a flaw to have only three in one of them, so the point count should be higher to compensate.

Responding to a Take-Out Double

Most players underestimate their hands when responding to a take-out double. They get nervous bidding so much on what they deem to be so little. The following is to help you judge your values.

Over one of a suit, suppose it was 1 Heart, your partner made a take-out double. What's your response?

With 0-5 points, you don't want to bid. You wish your partner hadn't doubled! So, if your right-hand opponent intervenes, pass. If he redoubles, you can also pass and let partner rescue himself. However, with no intervening bid, you must speak. Make the cheapest bid possible. Any four card suit is biddable. Generally, you bid your longest suit, but prefer a four-card major to a five-card minor. With ♠ Qxxx ♡xxx ◊ Kxxxx ♣x, bid 1 Spade, rather than 2 Diamonds.

With 6-9, you have a fair hand. Bid your best suit at the lowest level, even over an intervening bid. If the intervening bid happens to be your suit, double. That's a penalty double because your partner has bid.

With 10-12, you have a good hand. Take drastic action because there is an excellent chance for game. *Jump.* Bid one more than necessary even if your suit isn't robust. This jump is encouraging, but not forcing if partner has a minimum. With ♠ Qxxx ♡xx ◊ Axxx ♣ KJx, *jump* to 2 Spades.

With 13 high-cards points, and four cards in a unbid major, *jump to game.* With ♠ Axxx ♡xx ◊ KQx ♣KJxx, bid 4 Spades.

Partner's take-out double asks you to bid your best suit, but you may wish to bid No Trump with a balanced hand and the opponent's suit safely stopped — preferably twice. (With four cards in an unbid major, prefer the major.)

> With 8-10, bid 1 No Trump
> With 11-12, jump to 2 No Trump
> With 13-14, jump to 3 No Trump

You see, the No Trump response shows definite value.* It isn't bid just because you have a big card in the opponent's

---

*Notice this shows the same assets as bidding a No Trump after partner overcalls. See Chapter VIII.

suit. After partner doubled 1 Heart, holding ♠xxx ♡KJxx ◊ xxx ♣xxx, bid 1 Spade.

No matter how bad your hand, it is urgent for you to bid. Do not pass a take-out double because you have a weak hand and are scared. Passing in this situation is an aggressive action. It shows a desire to conquer the enemy on his own ground. (It asks for a trump lead!) The time to pass a take-out double is when you have a good hand and your best suit is the opponent's. At the 1-level, you need five tricks and three of them should be in trumps.

North	Partner	South	You
1♡	Double	Pass	?

(1) ♠ xx
   ♡ AJ109x
   ◊ KQx
   ♣ QJx

(2) ♠KQxx
   ♡AQ1094
   ◊ x
   ♣QJ9

(1) Partner wants you to bid a Spade but you have a doubleton. You would rather play Hearts than anything else. Pass. You have the requirements: 3 trump tricks + 1 Diamond trick + 1 Club trick. Partner's values for a take-out double will produce 2 or 3 tricks.

(2) You have the opponent's suit, but you have a fit with your partner. Prefer 4 Spades.

Rebids by the Take-Out Doubler

The take-out doubler, having forced his partner to bid, thereafter treads gently. If partner made a minimum response, that is, a non-jump bid:

With 13-15 and usually 16, pass. You've already bid your points. There is no game if partner doesn't have 10 points. Any further bid by you indicates game is still possible.

With 17-18 and four trumps, give a single raise to invite game.

With 19-21 and four trumps, give a jump raise.

However, when partner jumps the bidding to show 10 points, the doubler simply adds the combined hands. Suppose over 1 Heart you made a take-out double and your partner responded 2 Spades. Now what would you say holding:

(1) ♠ AJxx	(2) ♠ A10xx	(3) ♠ KQxx
♡ x	♡ xx	♡ xx
◊ KQxx	◊ KJ10x	◊ QJxx
♣ KJxx	♣ KQ10	♣ AQx

(1) Valued as a supporting hand you have 17 points; bid 4 Spades.

(2) You have a minimum take-out double. Valued as a dummy you have 14 points. Bid no more. You've bid your hand to the hilt.

(3) Valued as a supporting hand you have 15 points. Bid 3 Spades to urge partner to bid game with any extras over 10 points.

2. Too Strong To Overcall

With the upper limit of a 1-level overcall set at 15 points, it is necessary to find a way to show a stronger hand. This is the second use of the take-out double.

The handling of this hand is one of the distinguishing marks of the expert. He knows exactly how to bid it. Let his right-hand opponent open 1 Heart; it's the expert's turn to bid next. He holds ♠AKQxxx ♡xx ◊xx ♣AKx. The hand values at 18 points. How does he show it?

The expert makes a take-out double, and when the bidding comes back to him, bids Spades. When he made a take-out double asking partner to name a trump suit, and then he changed it and bid his own suit, he said, "I was too strong to overcall. I have more than 15 points."

Whereas, the average player, not knowing what to do, makes a simple overcall, and later wonders how he and partner could have found their game.

Look at these:

(1) ♠ AQ1098	(2) ♠ AQJ10x	(3) ♠ KQx
♡ xx	♡ x	♡ AQx
◊ K10x	◊ AKx	◊ K109
♣ AQJ	♣ Axxx	♣ AQxx

(1) Over 1 Heart a simple overcall of 1 Spade does not describe your strength. Double for take-out. If partner happens to respond in your suit, give a single raise. If he bids another suit, for instance 2 Clubs, bid 2 Spades. You asked partner to name the trump suit and then you changed it; this shows a medium hand of 16-18.

(2) Here you have a hand worth 20 points. Make a take-out double and at your next turn to bid, *jump* the bidding. If partner bids a Spade, *jump* to 3 Spades. If he bids 2 Clubs or 2 Diamonds, *jump* to 3 Spades. The *jump* shows 19-21 and distinguishes the maximum from a medium hand.

(3) You have a balanced hand and 20 points. You're too strong to overcall 1 No Trump. Make a take-out double. Next time around, bid No Trump at the lowest level. This shows 19-20 points, even distribution and a Heart stopper.

The bidding would go:

South	You	North	Partner
1 ♡	Double	Pass	1 ♠
Pass	1 NT		

Responding to a Take-out Double

With 0-9 bid longest suit at lowest level

With 10-12 jump one level

With 13 jump to game in a major

With even distribution, no biddable major, protection in opponent's suit:

    With 8-10 bid 1 NT

    With 11-12 jump to 2 NT

    With 13 jump to 3 NT

Rebids by the Take-out Doubler

If partner jumped, add your hand to his.
    Otherwise:

    With 13-15, usually 16, pass

    With 17-18 and four trumps, give a single raise

    With 19-21 and four trumps, give a jump raise

If partner didn't bid your suit:

    With 16-18 name a new suit

    With 19-21 jump one level in new suit

Tip

Your partner's double of 1 No Trump shows 16-18 points, the same as an opening No Trump. It is primarily for penalties. You add the assets and if you and your partner hold more than half the deck (22 or more), leave the double in. With less, rescue in your best suit.

The double of 2 No Trump is always for penalties, usually made with a long suit which can be quickly established, and an outside entry.

The double of a 3-bid in a suit is primarily for take-out but at this high level discretion may be exercised. A pass converts it to a penalty double.

The double of a bid of 4 Spades is primarily for penalties.

After partner has bid, all doubles are for penalties.

* * The Cue-Bid * *

Sometimes you pick up that elusive, big hand that calls for the **Two-Demand**, but before you get a chance to bid, an opponent opens the auction. The strong two-bid is no longer available to you. Still, you don't want to barge into your game, giving up slam possibility. Perhaps you have two suits and want partner to choose between them.

What can you do?

The strongest of all defensive bids is to repeat the opponent's suit — Opponent, "1 Heart"; You, "2 Hearts". It's called a cue-bid and promises enough power in your hand alone to bring in a game. It's forcing. Partner must respond, and keep responding, until game is reached.

When first devised by Ely Culbertson, the cue-bid also guaranteed first-round control of the enemy suit. Later, it evolved to second-round control. That stipulation fell by the wayside as the bid developed into such a useful tool. Today, it says nothing about your holding in the opponent's suit. It says, "I have a game-going hand. Bid!" Here are some examples to practice on. Your opponent opened 1 Heart. You're next. What would you bid holding:

(1) ♠ AKQ104   (2) ♠ AQJ   (3) ♠ AKQJ9872
    ♡ 8   ♡ ---   ♡ 4
    ◊ AKQ653   ◊ AJ10   ◊ AK
    ♣ 7   ♣ AKJ9875   ♣ 62

(1) Cue-bid 2 Hearts to guarantee an opportunity to send both your messages — that you have Spades and Diamonds. The auction might go:

South	You	North	Partner
1♡	2♡	Pass	3♣
Pass	3♠	Pass	4♣
Pass	4◊	Pass	5◊

Partner's hand could be, ♠x ♡xxx ◊xxxx ♣KJxxx. Without your cue-bid he wouldn't bid at all.

(2) The best spot for this one might be 5 Clubs, but if partner holds five Spades and no Clubs, certainly Spades is better; with a couple of Heart stops, No Trump might be wiser. A cue-bid of 2 Hearts lets you investigate.

(3) You have game in your own hand but you don't want to rule out a slam. First, cue-bid 2 Hearts, and next time around bid 4 Spades. This shows a stronger hand than either an immediate jump to 4 Spades, or a take-out double followed by 4 Spades.

A cue-bid is a way to say in bridge parlance, "Partner, tell me something about your hand." It has been developed to a fine degree today. Sometimes it is used later in the auction. Here's a sequence:

South	You	North	Partner
1♣	Double	Pass	2♣ Cue-bid

Your take-out double asked partner to bid a suit. (Of course you'd always prefer a major suit.) Now, partner cue-bids the opponent's suit! He's saying he has both majors, at least four cards in each, and sufficient high cards for game. He asks the doubler to name his stronger major. This is for safety's sake in case the doubler happens to hold only three cards in one of the majors.

Sometimes the opponents will rob you of your Stayman 2 Club bid:

Partner	South	You	North
1 NT	2 ◊	?	

You hold ♠ Kxxx ♡ QJxx ◊ x ♣ Qxxx. You'd planned to initiate the Stayman convention. Then South butt in. The 2-Club bid is no longer available. A cue-bid of the opponent's suit — a bid of 3 Diamonds — says, "Partner, tell me something about your hand." The "something" you want to know is, "Did you open a No Trump with a four-card major?"

Now the No Trump bidder can answer "3 Hearts" if he has four cards in the Heart suit, "3 Spades" with four cards in that suit, and "3 No Trump" to deny either. (Notice he was robbed of the negative Diamond reply. The bidding got too high.)

When your partner makes a cue-bid, pause a moment to think. What does he want to know about your hand? You can figure it out. Then bid. Be sure you bid. Don't pass and leave your partner playing a contract in the enemy's best suit!

IX. Test Your Other Defensive Bids

The bidding has gone:

South	You	North	Partner
1 ♣	Pass	2 ♣	Double
Pass	?		

What would you bid with:

(1) ♠ QJxx
♡ K10xx
◊ Axxx
♣ x

(2) ♠ x
♡ Q10xx
◊ AKJx
♣ 10xxx

(3) ♠ Kxx
♡ xx
◊ Kxxx
♣ KJxx

(4) ♠ xxx
♡ xx
◊ xxxx
♣ Kxxx

The bidding:

South	You	North	Partner
1 ♣	Double	Pass	1 ♠
Pass	?		

Are you going to take any further actions?

(5) ♠ AKxx
♡ K109x
◊ A10xx
♣ x

(6) ♠ KQx
♡ AQ10x
◊ KJx
♣ AJx

(7) ♠ Kxxx
♡ KJxx
◊ AQxx
♣ x

(8) ♠ KQJ10
♡ AKx
◊ AJ109
♣ xx

The dealer bid 1 Spade. You're next. What do you say holding:

(9) ♠ ---
♡ AQJx
◊ KQJx
♣ AQJxx

(10) ♠ xx
♡ AQxxx
◊ Axxx
♣ AQ

(11) ♠ x
♡ QJxxx
◊ xx
♣ AKxxx

The bidding:

North	Partner	South	You
1 Diamond	Double	Pass	?

(12) You hold: ♠ Qxxx ♡ KQxx ◊ x ♣ AQxx. What do you bid?_____

33. South Sets a Trap

By Becky Levering

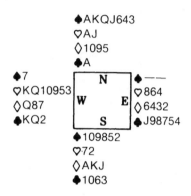

♠AKQJ643
♡AJ
◊1095
♣A

West:
♠7
♡KQ10953
◊Q87
♣KQ2

East:
♠——
♡864
◊6432
♣J98754

South:
♠109852
♡72
◊AKJ
♣1063

South deals

The bidding:

South	West	North	East
Pass	1 Heart	2 Hearts	Pass
3 Spades	Pass	4 NT	Pass
5 Diamonds	Pass	5 NT	Pass
6 Diamonds	Pass	6 Spades	All Pass

After West opened a Heart, North made the strongest bid he could make, cue-bidding the opponent's suit. Opposite this tremendous bid, South, with 8 high's and a five-card major, jumped to 3 Spades. North used Blackwood and settled in a 6 Spade contract. West led the Heart King.

South counted 11 tricks — seven Spades, two Diamonds, one Heart and one Club. His only source for a twelfth was Diamonds. Who had the Queen? North-South held 27 high-card points between them, leaving only 13 outstanding. West, the opening bidder, was marked with all of the missing face cards. He undoubtedly held the Diamond Queen. What could South do?

Then South saw a ray of light, and constructed a plan. He believed he could force West to lead Diamonds for him! He had the conditions for an end play — he could eliminate the side suits from the North-South hands and then throw West on lead, forcing a favorable return. Here is how he did it.

South won the Heart Ace and cashed the Club Ace. He led a small trump to his 10, and returned a Club, ruffing with a big trump. Another small trump was led to the 9 and declarer's last Club was ruffed on the board. Clubs had now been eliminated from both the North and South hands. Declarer led dummy's last Heart, the Jack, following with the last Heart in his own hand; West won the Queen. Hearts were now eliminated from the North-South hands. Now, South's trap is set:

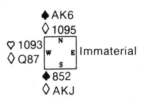

West was end-played. Any card he led would give South a trick and his slam. If he returned a Diamond, it would make a winner out of declarer's Jack. If he returned a Heart, declarer could ruff in one hand while discarding a losing Diamond in the other.

West tried to escape with the Diamond 7 (hoping partner held the Jack) but, alas, East dropped the deuce, and declarer won with the Jack. The rest were his. Mission accomplished.

34. Cue-bid Promises a Powerhouse

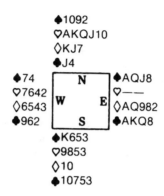

```
                ♠1092
                ♡AKQJ10
                ◊KJ7
                ♣J4
    ♠74          ┌─────────┐    ♠AQJ8
    ♡7642        │    N    │    ♡——
    ◊6543    W   │         │ E  ◊AQ982
    ♣962         │    S    │    ♣AKQ8
                 └─────────┘
                ♠K653
                ♡9853
                ◊10
                ♣10753
```

West deals

The bidding:

West	North	East	South
Pass	1 Heart	2 Hearts	Pass
3 Diamonds	Pass	5 Diamonds	All Pass

Poised to open with a Two-Demand, East heard his opponent call a Heart. East bid 2 Hearts! Holding the weakest hand at the table West came up with 3 Diamonds, and East contracted for an 11-trick game.

North opened the King of his powerful Heart suit. With a sick feeling declarer studied the dummy and gulped at the rough road ahead. He ruffed in dummy. He desperately wanted to get to his own miserable hand to finesse trumps. He cashed the Spade Ace and continued the Queen. South won his King and pursued with a Heart, forcing a second ruff in the big hand and bringing it down to three trumps.

With his heart in his throat, declarer led a low Spade and trumped it with the Diamond 3. It won! Now he led the Diamond 6, North covered with the 7, and declarer finessed the Queen. When South dropped the 10, declarer perked up. He persisted with the trump Ace and the Jack fell.

Declarer now made a key play. He led Diamonds no more. The outstanding trump was high and North could take it whenever he wished. West started cashing side winners, playing the A-K-Q of Clubs. On the last North swooped down with the trump King and led Hearts again. The battle was all over because dummy still held one trump. Furthermore, West still held a trump which he collected separately.

East's cue-bid of the opponent's suit was a gigantic take-out double, forcing to game. To use it your partner must know the bid. I heard it first 22 years ago. On my left the bishop's wife opened a Spade. My partner, a four-star general, bid 2 Spades. With a hand like West's, I pondered the meaning of the general's bid and decided the bishop's wife had psyched (bid a suit she didn't have). I passed. I can still see General Gab Dissosway write down the score in the "They" column. It was one of my many lessons in the School of Hard Knocks.

35. The Rule of Eleven Rides Again

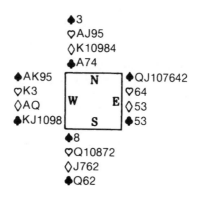

```
              ♠3
              ♡AJ95
              ◊K10984
              ♣A74
  ♠AK95     ┌─────────┐    ♠QJ107642
  ♡K3       │    N    │    ♡64
  ◊AQ       │ W     E │    ◊53
  ♣KJ1098   │    S    │    ♣53
            └─────────┘
              ♠8
              ♡Q10872
              ◊J762
              ♣Q62
```

North deals

The bidding:

North	East	South	West
1 Diamond	Pass	1 Heart	Double
2 Hearts	2 Spades	Pass	4 Spades
All Pass			

When the bidding revolved to West, he made a take-out double with 20 highs and excellent support for the unbid suits. North stepped in with a Heart raise, erasing the double, and East no longer was forced to respond. But East looked fondly at his long Spade suit and freely entered the auction. That was all the encouragement West needed. He went to game.

South led his fourth-best Heart, the 7. Declarer ducked in dummy. Using the Rule of Eleven, 11 - 7 = 4, North learned there were four outstanding Hearts higher than partner's. He could see all of them in his hand and dummy's. He played the 5 and South won the trick. Studying the dummy and remembering the bidding, South switched to a low Diamond. East tried the Queen but North won the King and cashed the Heart Ace. Eventually, he won the Club Ace to set the contract.

If North were to thoughtlessly win trick one, say with the Heart Jack, partner would never be on lead again to make the strategic Diamond lead. North could take his Heart Ace, but after that declarer would get in, pull trumps, and finesse Clubs. When the 8 forced the Ace, declarer, again, would win any return, and finesse Clubs a second time, winning the 9. Next, he would lead the Club King, discarding the losing Diamond in his own hand, and all the rest would be his and he would make his contract.

Back to trick one, if declarer should play dummy's Heart King, life is easy for the defenders. North wins the Ace and returns a low Heart. South wins, and shoots back a Diamond. Declarer's play of the low Heart was correct, and gave North a chance to go wrong, and this, in the long run is an important element in good card play.

Nevertheless, in the final analysis, it was the Rule of Eleven that sank the contract.

36. Bidding Over a Preempt

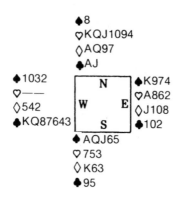

```
              ♠8
              ♡KQJ1094
              ◊AQ97
              ♣AJ
♠1032      ┌─────────┐   ♠K974
♡——        │    N    │   ♡A862
◊542       │ W     E │   ◊J108
♣KQ87643   │    S    │   ♣102
           └─────────┘
              ♠AQJ65
              ♡753
              ◊K63
              ♣95
```

East deals

The bidding:

East	South	West	North
Pass	Pass	3 Clubs	Double
Pass	4 Spades	Pass	4 NT
Pass	5 Diamonds	Pass	6 Hearts
All Pass			

West's preemptive call didn't keep North-South from zeroing into their little slam. After North's take-out double, South jumped to show 10 points. Now, North employed Blackwood, and climbed to 6 Hearts.

East led the Club 10. West pushed with the Queen, and declarer won the Ace. North stared at two immediate losers, the trump Ace and a Club. He had to get rid of that Club before the opponents got the lead with the trump Ace.

He laid down the Spade 8 and finessed dummy's Queen, which held the trick. Quickly, he played the Spade Ace to dump the Club loser.

Over that hurdle, he pulled trumps. East won the Ace and played a Club but North was now able to ruff. He brought in all the outstanding trumps. When the Diamonds divided nicely he won 12 tricks.

X. SIGNALING

The declarer is fortunate in that he gets to see all his partner's cards. He knows which suit to lead, from which hand he should initiate it, and with which card.

Not so for the poor, blind defender who sees only 13 of the cards for his side. Defense is difficult, but can be extremely exciting. It is urgent for the defending partners to guide each other. Over the years experienced players have developed a code by which defenders can send messages to each other by the order in which they play their small, inconsequential cards that cannot take a trick. They signal with them.

Like traffic lights some cards say, GO and some say STOP. A defender can tell his partner if he likes his opening lead, or if he'd like a switch to another suit . . . and sometimes even which suit. He can also tell partner how many cards he holds in a suit.

* * Attitude * *

The first and most important of all defensive signals is attitude.* How do you feel about partner's opening lead? Do you like it? or, do you wish him to play another suit? You can encourage him to continue the same suit by playing *an unnecessarily high card, a 6 or above,* which says, "I like that suit; keep leading it." Or, a 5 or lower which says, "I don't like that suit." When you choose your come-on card, be careful to keep a lower card to play to the second round of the suit. Playing your cards out of order — a high card first,

---

*Also dubbed the high-low signal, the come-on signal, or the echo.

then a low card next — is to attract attention. It is a recognized method of signaling your partner to keep leading that suit.

Here's how it works. Against a Spade contract your partner opened the Heart King. Which card would you play from these examples:

(1) **Partner** — **You**
♡K | ♡Q93

(2) **Partner** — **You**
♡K | ♡93

In (1) you play the 9 which says, "Come on with that suit," so partner obligingly next cashes the Heart Ace and you play the 3. (You played high, then low.) Now, he'll lead Hearts a third time so you can win your Queen. In (2) you play the same way for a different reason. This time you play high-low planning to win the third round by trumping.

(3) **Partner** — **You**
♡K | ♡J102

(4) **Partner** — **You**
♡K | ♡962

In (3) you play the 2 because you want partner to abandon the suit. You want to make the next Heart play yourself so if the declarer has the Queen you can trap it. In (4) you play the 2 because you have no help in the suit.

Sometimes you won't have picturesque cards for signaling. Then, do the best you can:

(5) **Partner** — **You**
♡K | ♡Q32

(6) **Partner** — **You**
♡K | ♡J98

In (5) you play the most encouraging card available, the Heart 3, and hope partner is alert, sees the 2 missing, and continues the suit. In (6) you got a bad deal again; you don't want partner to continue Hearts but your lowest card is the 8. It's going to look like a come-on card but you can't help it.

Just play the best you can. Most of the time you will find a descriptive card to send the message you want to send.

It's important to play your cards intelligently so your partner will form the habit of "reading" them. A card that cannot possibly win a trick can carry a message that will set a contract.

Sometimes you will hold a wealth of descriptive cards and can choose:

(7) **Partner** ♡K **You** ♡Q863   (8) **Partner** ♡K **You** ♡Q8642

In (7) you definitely wish Hearts continued and both the 8 and the 6 are encouraging. You should play the highest card you can afford, the 8, because it speaks louder. Some partners don't hear well. On the next go-round complete your story with the 3.

Although small cards show a lack of interest in a suit they show it in different degrees. In (8) the 2 says, "stop, switch." The 4, "I don't mind if you continue." The 6, "Please continue Hearts." The 8, "Partner, keep coming with those Hearts!"

The expert plays his 2's as carefully as he plays his Kings. When he says STOP he wants a switch; he has an interest in another suit. With an empty hand he might play a mildly encouraging 4. Sometimes, fearing a damaging shift, he might play the 6 for a come-on even though he doesn't have anything in the suit.

Although discouraging cards tell partner you cannot help in that suit and you advise a shift, with a solid suit partner will continue leading it anyway. When he knows something that he's sure you don't know, he can veto your recommendation.

Discards

You can also flash a signal when you cannot follow suit. You can make an informative discard by playing an ostentatious card in the suit you wish led — a 6 or above — and then a lower card. This opportunity frequently arises while declarer is pulling trumps. Against a 4 Heart contract you hold:

♠AK62 ♡7 ◇J5432 ♣J42

Partner opened a low Club, which was won in dummy as you followed with the 2. Next, declarer played three rounds of Hearts. On the first, you followed. On the next, you played the Spade 6, and on the third round, you completed your story with the Diamond 2. If partner happens to win the lead, he'll know to lead a Spade for you.

Here you could afford to discard the Spade 6. Sometimes you don't have that luxury. Suppose your Spades were AKQ2. You don't want to signal with one of your honors because you'd be throwing a winner. Be imaginative. You can send the same message by inference by playing low cards in the other suits. Discard the Diamond deuce to say, "I have no interest in Diamonds." An alert partner will reason that if you don't like Clubs and you don't like Diamonds, you must want a Spade lead. You would discard a Spade honor as a signal only in case of an emergency.

Sometimes the declarer will run a long suit hoping to get the defenders to discard wrong. It is urgent for defenders to signal each other which suit they can protect by playing high-low. They play in a normal fashion discarding a suit they can't protect. This avoids both saving the same suit.

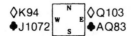

While South runs his eight-card trump suit East and West are thrown into a tizzy, each holding vital cards in both minors. West should discard the Diamond 9 telling partner he can protect that suit, freeing East from having to protect the Diamond Queen. East should discard the Club 8 promising he has control there, freeing West to throw Clubs. East will complete his echo with the Club 3, but West cannot afford to complete his echo.

Never signal with a card that will take a trick. That's too expensive. Signaling is important but taking tricks is the soul of the game.

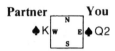

Partner   **You**

♠K   ♠Q2

In the example, partner opens the Spade King. You play the 2 because the Queen will take a trick. You hope partner abandons the suit; when you later get in, you can lead the Queen yourself, and partner can follow with a baby Spade.

Actually *the discard of a Queen carries a special message.* It is an accepted convention that against a suit contract if a player leads a King and partner follows with the Queen it is a command that the opening leader, at the very next trick, lead a small card in that suit. He must in no case cash his Ace. When a player throws an honor on a trick, which that honor cannot win, he promises he holds the card below it.

(1) **Partner**   **You**   (2) **Partner**   **You**

♠K   ♠QJ   ♠K   ♠QJ72

In (1) you drop the Queen to ask partner to lead a low Spade so your honors won't crash together. If you played the Jack partner would read it as a come-on and continue the Ace and the Queen would fall.

When it is obvious your honor card cannot possibly win a trick you might signal with it to gain the lead at a strategic moment. Suppose your partner bid Diamonds and Spades but the opponents won the auction. On opening lead partner lays down the Spade King. You see dummy has only two Spades. You want to win the next trick so you can play Diamonds through declarer. In (2) you play the Queen to ask for a low Spade continuation. You will win with your Jack and make the Diamond play.

To summarize:

• Encourage by following with a high card — a 6 or above — and next play a lower one.

• Discourage by following low.

• In discarding, if you can afford it, play high-low in the suit you wish led. Conversely, throw a low card in a suit you don't want led.

• Discarding a Queen commands the immediate lead of a small card in that suit.

• Signaling by inference. When you can't relinquish a card in the suit you wish led, discard low cards in the suits you don't want.

*   *   **Falsecarding by the Declarer**   *   *

What is the declarer doing while the defenders are "talking" across the table? He observes all, and sometimes it helps him to locate a vital card. Nevertheless, the signals are of greater assistance to the defense.

If the declarer uses the same signals in exactly the same manner as the defenders he can sometimes garble the defender's code! He, too, should play high-low when he wants a suit continued and low when he doesn't. This falsecarding by the declarer is foxy. See for yourself:

(1)
♠863
N
W   E
S
♠KQ109   ♠74
♠AJ52

(2)
♠765
N
W   E
S
♠AK108   ♠J94
♠Q32

In (1) West, leading against a No Trump contract, laid down the Spade King. East played his lowest Spade, the 4, to warn partner against continuing. Declarer was planning to duck this trick, but he yearned for West to play Spades again because it would give him an extra trick. Therefore, declarer played his 5, concealing the 2. South hoped West would note the 2 missing and think East had something like J42 or A42 and was trying to coax West to continue the suit. Notice how easy it is for West to read his partner's card if declarer plays the 2.

In (2) West, leading against a suit contract, opened the Spade King and partner warned him not to continue the suit by playing the 4. Declarer wanted it continued so he falsecarded with the 3, hoping to make East's card look like a come-on.

The corollary is also true. Declarer plays his smallest card when he doesn't want a suit continued, just as though he were a defender giving attitude. Again, it will sometimes confuse the defender on lead.

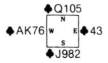

♠Q105
N
W   E
S
♠AK76   ♠43
♠J982

Against a Spade contract West led the Club King and partner signaled come-on the best he could with the 4; he wanted to trump the third round. South's best chance to stop the continuation was to play the 2, hoping West would think East had something like J94.

If declarer has to stop and figure out each falsecard he might forewarn defenders he's doing just that. The hoax is more likely to succeed if you play quickly. The champions have already figured it out for you; save your thinking for more complicated plays. Attempting to disrupt the opponents' signaling use the same method yourself.

* * The Count Signal * *

When the declarer is running a long suit the high-low signal to show attitude becomes useless. Obviously, if declarer is attacking a suit, he has the power in it. Therefore, when declarer is leading a suit the defenders can use the high-low signal to give another kind of information. They can use it to indicate how many cards they have in that suit. It's called "giving the count," or the Count Signal. You show *an odd number of cards by playing naturally,* from the bottom up, advertising one, three, or five cards in the suit. You show *an even number of cards by playing unnaturally,* a high and then a low card announcing two, four, or six cards. This enables the defenders to calculate how many cards declarer holds in a specific suit. This is useful knowledge when one defender holds a big card in declarer's strong suit and wants to win it at the most opportune moment. An often recurring instance is when dummy has a long suit and no other entry:

```
                    ◇ KQ1064
         Partner ┌─────────┐ You
                 │    N    │
         ◇ 75    │ W     E │ ◇ A93
                 │    S    │
                 └─────────┘
                    ◇ J82
```

Declarer led the Diamond Jack, West played the 7 beginning the high-low signal to show an even number of cards in the suit. East ducked. Declarer continued the 2 and West completed his story with the Diamond 5. By adding his cards and dummy's, East realized declarer had three cards in the suit and held up one more round, limiting declarer to two Diamond tricks. If East had won his Ace on the first or the second round, declarer could have taken four Diamond tricks. By denying declarer access to his last two winners East and West — working together — moved toward setting the contract.

Let's play that hand once more but re-deal the Diamonds and give West one more, the 752, and declarer the doubleton J8. Now when declarer leads the suit West first plays the 2, the next round the 5, showing an odd number of cards. East can count the Diamonds in his hand and dummy to deduce West has specifically three. That tells him declarer holds only two. East wins the second round, killing the dummy at the precise moment declarer can no longer reach it.

High-Low Echo in Trumps

In the trump suit the count signal is reversed. When a defender follows high-low it shows an odd number, usually three. Playing normally shows an even number, two or four.

Signals are attention-getters. Playing high-low in trumps is primarily to alert partner you wish to trump something and you have another trump. It's important for partner to know this so he can try to give you a ruff with the third one.

* * Suit Preference Signals * *

When it is impossible for a signal to be showing attitude, or count, it is a Suit Preference Signal, one of the most exciting plays in all of bridge. It's a way to tell your partner which suit you want him to play next. This is most often used when a ruff is involved.

1. Singleton in Dummy: Suppose the opening lead is a suit in which dummy produces a singleton. A switch is called for; defenders don't like the dummy ruffing. The defender in third seat can tell his partner which side suit he likes by the size of the card he plays! Would you like to see it at work?

You bid a Spade but the opponents outbid you in Hearts. On opening lead partner played the Spade King and dummy came down:

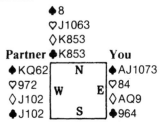

♠8
♡J1063
◊K853
Partner ♣K853 You

♠KQ62 ♠AJ1073
♡972   ♡84
◊J102 ◊AQ9
♣J102 ♣964

Obviously, dummy is going to ruff the next Spade and your partner is going to play something else. He doesn't know whether to lead a Diamond or a Club. *The size of the card you play* tells whether you want the higher-ranking side suit or the lower-ranking side suit. For this message trumps are eliminated, and the suit dummy is trumping is eliminated. Only two suits are involved, Diamonds and Clubs. Following with a high card like a Jack requests a Diamond and a low card like the 3 asks for a Club. High for high, low for low. On this hand you'd play the Jack of Spades (this is not a time to be thrifty; make the message clear) and partner would comply by laying down the Jack of Diamonds. You set declarer before he gets in. Any other play, a Spade continuation or a Club or a trump, would give declarer time to pull trumps and discard one losing Diamond from his hand, making his contract.

Notice that dummy's holding in Clubs and Diamonds is identical. Which to lead is a guess. The convention was devised to eliminate doubt. West had nothing to guide him, until the Jack of Spades came down, a beacon of light.

The Suit Preference Signal applied because it was quite evident another Spade lead was not desired. Common sense dictated it couldn't be a come-on signal.

2. **A Signal to the Ruffer:** Another opportunity for the Suit Preference Signal arises when you're leading a suit you know partner is going to ruff. The size of the card you lead is a signal to tell him where you have an entry, so you can give him another ruff. If the card is an unnecessarily high one, it suggests the higher-ranking of the two remaining side suits. If the card is a low one, it suggests the lower-ranking suit. Here it is:

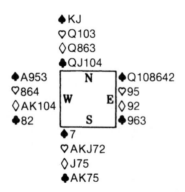

Against four Hearts you led your Diamond King. Although continuing the suit would set up dummy's Queen, partner asked you to play it again by laying down the Diamond 9, obviously a come-on card. You play the Diamond Ace and partner completes his signal with the Diamond 2. You know he's planning to ruff the third round. You have a choice of cards to play. Should you play the Diamond 10 or the 4? It's important. Each carries a different message. The 10 asks for the higher-ranking side suit to be returned (Spades) and the 4 asks for the lower-ranking (Clubs). Again, trumps are eliminated from the picture and the suit being led is eliminated. Since you hold the Spade Ace, you lead the Diamond 10. Partner trumps and returns a Spade. You win the Ace and return another Diamond so partner can trump the ranking Diamond Queen. True, declarer will overruff but he won't get a free discard.

If your partner had to guess, and happened to guess a Club, declarer would win the Club Ace, pull trumps, and then throw his losing Spade on the Diamond Queen which the defense turned into a winner.

3. **To Show an Entry When Running a Long Suit:** Another time for this illuminating play is when you're leading a long suit against No Trump. You know partner is depleted of your suit and you want to tell him where you have an entry.

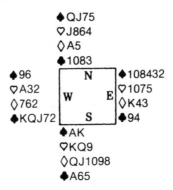

Against 3 No Trump you opened the Club King, and declarer held up (our old friend the ducking play at work!). You won and played the Club Queen. Again declarer held back his Ace. Eight Clubs have been played; you see three in your hand and one in dummy. There is only one not visible, the Ace, and declarer must have it. Any Club you play will

bring it down. Play the one that tells your partner where you have an entry.

Here three suits are involved. (Clubs are out of the picture because partner hasn't any.) A big Club, the Jack, says lead the highest of high, a Spade; the 7 calls for the middle suit, Hearts; the 2 asks for a Diamond.

You play the 7. Declarer wins the Club Ace, then finesses the Diamond Queen. East wins, returns a Heart, and down goes South. If East had to guess and guessed a Spade, declarer could gallop off with nine tricks.

To summarize:

• When your partner leads a suit you show attitude.

• When the declarer leads a suit you give count; you play high-low with an even number of cards and normally with an odd number of cards. Reverse the signal in trumps.

• When it is impossible for a signal to be construed as attitude or count, it's the suit preference signal.

Tip

Don't let occasional errors discourage you. Experts sometimes misread a signal. When your signaling goes astray, discuss it with your partner and try to analyze what went wrong. Or, write it down and consult the best player you know. Signaling will make the game much more exciting for you. Instead of woodenly following suit, learn to talk with your immaterial cards.

X. Test Your Signaling

(1)

```
              ♠K104
              ♡K3
              ◇Q43
              ♣AKQJ6
♠95       ┌─────────┐
♡A52      │    N    │
◇AKJ72    │ W     E │
♣975      │    S    │
          └─────────┘
```

As West you open the Diamond King against a 4 Spade contract. Partner plays the Diamond 9.

(a) What do you play next? Then what? Any chance of setting declarer?

(b) Suppose you held six Diamonds. Now what are your chances?

(2)

```
              ♠K952
              ♡A4
              ◇J987
              ♣1092
          ┌─────────┐  ♠Q74
          │    N    │  ♡Q972
          │ W     E │  ◇K4
          │    S    │  ♣J854
          └─────────┘
```

Against 3 No Trump, West leads the Heart 5 and declarer goes up with dummy's Ace. What card should East play?

(3)

```
              ♠73
              ♡KQ10
              ◇KQJ974
              ♣A9
♠AKJ106   ┌─────────┐
♡852      │    N    │
◇A        │ W     E │
♣J743     │    S    │
          └─────────┘
```

Against 3 No Trump, West leads the Spade King and East plays the 2. What card should West play next?

182

(4)

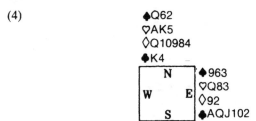

(a) West leads the Heart 9 against 3 No Trump. Declarer plays dummy's King. What card should East play?

(b) Declarer next leads a low Diamond. What card should East play?

(c) On the third round of Diamonds, East cannot follow suit. What card should he play?

(5)

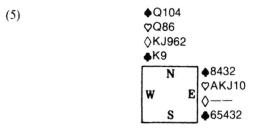

Partner opens the Diamond 5 against 3 No Trump. What card should East play to trick one? Declarer leads another round of Diamonds. What card should East play?

(6)

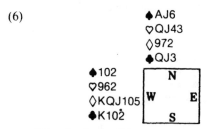

West leads the Diamond King against 3 No Trump. It wins, and he continues the Queen, which also holds. Everyone follows. What card should West play next?

(7)

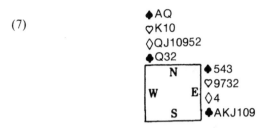

```
        ♠AQ
        ♡K10
        ◇QJ10952
        ♣Q32
    ┌─────────┐    ♠543
    │    N    │    ♡9732
    │ W     E │    ◇4
    │    S    │    ♣AKJ109
    └─────────┘
```

West opens a small Spade against 3 No Trump. Declarer wins dummy's Queen and plays a Diamond to his Ace and King. What card should East discard on the second Diamond trick?

(8)

```
            ◇964
         ┌────────┐
◇ AK75   │ N      │   ◇ J103
         │ W    E │
         │   S    │
         └────────┘
            ◇ Q82
```

Against 3 Spades, West leads the Diamond King. What card should East play? What card should declarer (South) play? Why?

(9)

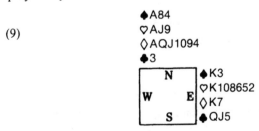

```
        ♠A84
        ♡AJ9
        ◇AQJ1094
        ♣3
    ┌─────────┐    ♠K3
    │    N    │    ♡K108652
    │ W     E │    ◇K7
    │    S    │    ♣QJ5
    └─────────┘
```

North bid a Diamond, East overcalled a Heart, and South wound up in 4 Spades. West led the Heart Queen and declarer went up with dummy's Ace. Declarer played the trump Ace and then a low trump, West following with the 7, and then the 2. East captures the second trump; what does he play? Then what?

37. It Takes Two to Tango

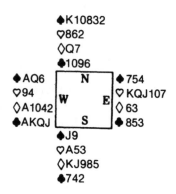

South deals

The bidding:

South	West	North	East
Pass	1 Club	Pass	1 Heart
Pass	3 NT	Pass	All Pass

As soon as East mentioned Hearts, West, with 20 high card-points, was ready to bid the No Trump game. North led his fourth-best Spade, the 3. South protected with the Jack, and declarer won the Queen.

West went into a huddle and found seven ready-made tricks. He needed two more and he saw a rich source in dummy's solid Hearts. He pulled out his Heart 9. Now, North walked to center stage and played the informative Heart 2. South ducked, allowing the 9 to win. Declarer continued with another Heart, North followed with the 6, and South pounced on this one with his Ace. Then, South leaned back in his chair, relaxed, and returned partner's Spade suit.

Declarer took his Spade Ace, rattled off his four Clubs, cashed the Diamond Ace, and gave up. He was down one. He had three heart winners in dummy and no way to reach them.

How did South know to take his Heart Ace on the second round? Why didn't he wait for the third go-round and be sure declarer couldn't get to dummy?

North told him! North told his partner he had an odd number of Hearts by playing his cards naturally, from the bottom up. (He would have echoed by playing a high card and then a low card, the 6 and then the 2, with an even number of cards in Hearts.) Thus South was able to deduce his partner had exactly three Hearts; with dummy showing five and his own three, South figured declarer held only two. He killed the dummy at the precise moment to hold declarer to a minimum.

West had a contract of 3 No Trump. North-South had a contract, too; it was to set 3 No Trump. It took perfect card play by two people.

38. Hearing What the Small Cards Say

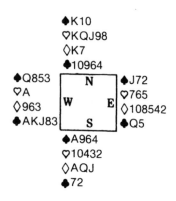

```
              ♠K10
              ♡KQJ98
              ◊K7
              ♣10964
♠Q853          N          ♠J72
♡A                        ♡765
◊963      W        E      ◊108542
♣AKJ83         S          ♣Q5
              ♠A964
              ♡10432
              ◊AQJ
              ♣72
```

West deals

The bidding

West	North	East	South
1 Club	1 Heart	Pass	3 Hearts
Pass	4 Hearts	All Pass	

East led the Club Queen, which captured trick one, and continued another to partner's Jack. West stepped out with his top Club. North followed, and East trumped his partner's Ace (!) with the Heart 6. No problem. Dummy overruffed with the Heart 10.

North counted his tricks — four Hearts, three Diamonds, two Spades, and the Club he had just ruffed equaled 10. He was home. Pulling a low Heart from dummy, he went after trumps. West, perforce, won the Ace, and saw his partner echo with the Heart 5.

Book-in, the defenders needed just one more trick. West played the Club King. Falteringly, North followed with the Club 10, as he began to sense the horror ahead. East trumped with the Heart 7, and dummy couldn't beat it. Declarer got the rest, but he was down one.

Bridge players have long thought they'd be struck by a bolt of lightening if they trumped their partner's Ace. It has been the subject of many cartoons. According to legend, it once drove a man to commit murder. (The judge was sympathetic and ruled it involuntary manslaughter.) But our East was looking ahead.

"Thanks for trumping my Ace and King of Clubs," West smiled in approval. "Your trump echo, telling me you were eager to ruff something, was a dramatic signal."

"Partner," complained South, "you're the eternal optimist. Before leading trumps, why not play Diamonds and drop that burdensome Club 10. Now, when West gets in with the trump Ace and plays a Club, *you* can ruff. Your lowest Heart tops East's. You gave yourself one chance — that the Hearts were evenly divided. You could have given yourself two."

North was stony silent.

39. Every Card Carried a Message

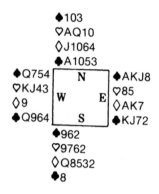

```
              ♠103
              ♡AQ10
              ◊J1064
              ♣A1053
♠Q754    ┌─────────┐   ♠AKJ8
♡KJ43    │    N    │   ♡85
◊9       │ W     E │   ◊AK7
♣Q964    │    S    │   ♣KJ72
         └─────────┘
              ♠962
              ♡9762
              ◊Q8532
              ♣8
```

North deals

The bidding:

North	East	South	West
Pass	1 Club	Pass	1 Heart
Pass	2 Spades	Pass	3 Spades
Pass	4 Spades	All Pass	

On lead with such a pitiful holding, South could see only one way he could help defeat declarer — to get a ruff — so he opened his singleton Club. Up popped North with the Ace. Reading the lead for a singleton, he studied his choices for a Club return, 10 - 5 - 3.

North had an inside advantage because he knew the Club he chose would be interpreted as a suit preference signal to alert partner wherein his future re-entry lay. For his signal, Spades are eliminated because they're trumps, and Clubs are eliminated because partner hasn't any; only Hearts and Diamonds are involved. The clue is in the size of the card North returns; a high card asks for the higher-ranking suit and a low card for the lower-ranking suit.

Carefully, North chose the Club 10. South stepped up with the Spade 6, and then, conforming to partner's request, played a Heart. Declarer chose dummy's Jack, and North won with the Heart Queen. He returned another Club. South trumped meticulously with the Spade 2, completing his *trump echo*, and continued Hearts. Dummy's King was captured by North's Ace.

Now, North stood at the cross-roads. Did partner have another trump? Or, should North try to cash the ranking Heart 10?

North didn't have to guess! Partner had eloquently proclaimed he held a third trump when he echoed. So, North persisted with another Club and watched partner win with the Spade 9. South tried Hearts again, but East trumped. Finally in the lead, declarer raked in the rest of the tricks.

At trick one a strong and mighty East counted only three losers, but North-South's deft defense multiplied them to six, crumbling the contract the maximum. Down three!

40. East Can Afford It

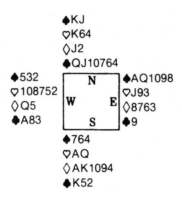

```
                    ♠KJ
                    ♡K64
                    ◇J2
                    ♣QJ10764
      ♠532            N          ♠AQ1098
      ♡108752                    ♡J93
      ◇Q5         W       E      ◇8763
      ♣A83            S          ♣9
                    ♠764
                    ♡AQ
                    ◇AK1094
                    ♣K52
```

East deals

The bidding:

East	South	West	North
Pass	1 NT	Pass	3 NT
All Pass			

With 16 gilt-edge points, even distribution, and three suits protected, South opened a No Trump and his partner cheerfully carried him to game with 11 highs and a beautiful Club suit.

West opened his fourth-best Heart, the 5. Dummy played low, East went up with the Jack, and declarer won the Ace. South could count five Club tricks, two Diamonds, and two or three Hearts, which would give him his contract with an overtrick. He headed for the longest suit first and laid down the Club King. West held back his Ace; he could see he wasn't going to lose it with that long suit in dummy and he wanted to see what his partner had to say. Declarer's King won as East contributed the 9. (To West, of course, that 9 looked like the beginning of the count signal to show a doubleton.)

Another Club hit the table. West climbed up with his Ace, and saw East, unable to follow suit, play the Spade 10. It was obviously a come-on card, clearly marking the road for West. Quickly, he led the Spade 5. Dummy played the Jack, and East pranced out with the Queen. Next, East brought out the Spade Ace to pick up the King. He played two more Spade winners to put declarer down one.

It was urgent for East to show the way. If he had hoarded his Spades, hoping to win every single one of them, South would have walked away with 10 tricks. A low Diamond discard could be misunderstood. It could be interpreted as a desire for a Heart continuation. East could afford to signal with the Spade 10 because he still held enough Spade tricks to sink the contract.

ANSWERS TO TESTS

I. Card Plays

(1) Lead a low card from your hand and insert the 10. If that loses to the Jack (or wins the trick) come back to your hand in another suit. Again, lead toward the dummy, and risk the Queen.

(2) To win three tricks, play the King, then lead low from dummy and finesse the Jack.

(3) To win two tricks, lead the 10 from your hand and let it ride. If that loses to the Jack, get back in your hand (with another suit), lead the Queen, and let it ride.

(4) To win two tricks, lead from dummy and finesse the 10. The next time lead again from dummy and finesse the Jack.

(5) To win two tricks, lead from your hand and finesse the 10. If that loses to the Ace, get back in your hand, lead low, and finesse the Jack.

(6) Lead the Queen from dummy. If East covers, you cover. If East plays low, you play low. If the Queens wins, repeat the finesse.

(7) Hoping to win one trick, lead a low card from dummy. If East plays low, put in the Jack. Assuming that loses to West's Ace (or King), when you're back in dummy, lead low again *toward* your honor. If East plays low, put up the Queen. Whenever the Ace and King are divided (50% of the time) you can win a trick, or whenever East has both (25% of the time) you'll win one.

(8) First lead low from dummy; if East plays low, go up with the Queen. If East plays the King, you play low.

(9) First, cash the Ace. Then lead low from dummy *toward* your QJx. If East plays the King, you play low. If East plays low, you go up with an honor. If this honor wins, go back to dummy in another suit and repeat.

(10) Play low and play casually. East shouldn't cover with the King. There's no chance to set up a card for yourself or partner. Declarer has all of them.

(11) Low. Cover dummy's last honor.

(12) Cover with the King.

(13) Play low, and at an even tempo. Keep your hand steady. Don't let your eyebrows twitch.

II. No Trump, Stayman, and Gerber

(1) Bid 2 Clubs. If partner answers 2 Spades bid 4 Spades; if he answers 2 Diamonds or 2 Hearts bid 3 No Trump. Conceal a long minor.

(2) Bid 2 Clubs. If partner says 2 Hearts give a single raise to 3 Hearts showing 8 or 9 points. If partner answers 2 Spades or 2 Diamonds bid 2 No Trump, just as you would if you'd never employed Stayman.

(3) Jump to 3 No Trump. Don't use Stayman without a distributional point.

(4) Bid 2 Spades, a rescue. It will be easier to land eight tricks at Spades than seven tricks at No Trump.

(5) Jump to 3 Hearts and let partner choose the final contract of 4 Hearts or 3 No Trump.

(6) Bid 6 No Trump. You see it, go.

(7) Bid 2 Clubs, Stayman. If partner answers 2 Spades or 2 Hearts, your hand values at 10, bid 4. If he bids 2 Diamonds, bid 2 Spades showing a five-card suit and 8 or 9 points.

(8) Pass. The hand might play better at Clubs, but your partner will take it as the Stayman convention.

(9) Bid 2 Spades. Just answer the question. You don't like your Spade holding and you can't ruff anything, but your partner is the captain.

(10) Bid 2 Diamonds. It's artificial, has nothing to do with the Diamond suit.

(11) Double for penalties. You're going to get rich. Your side has at least 26 points. Declarer won't have an entry to dummy and will have to play everything out of his hand.

(12) Bid 3 Spades. When you bid the opponent's suit it's a cue bid, asking partner to tell you something about his hand. Here's you're using it for Stayman to ask if partner has a four-card Heart suit; the opponent robbed you of your 2 Club bid. You want to reach game but you're not certain whether you want to play it in No Trump or Hearts.

(13) Bid 4 Clubs (Gerber) asking for Aces. If partner answers 4 Diamonds showing all, bid 7 Diamonds. If partner answers 4 No Trump showing three Aces, settle for 6 Diamonds.

(14) Bid 3 Clubs, Stayman. Over 2 No Trump you need only four points for Stayman.

III. Ducking Plays

(1) The Heart Ace and then a small Heart from each hand, ducking one round. West needs four Heart tricks to bring in his contract and plays for a 3-2 split. He holds back

the Heart King until the third round because it's his only entry to the long suit.

(2) Win the Ace and run with nine tricks. Ducking would risk a switch to a more dangerous suit, Spades.

(3) The Club King. Let partner's Hearts wait. The first order of business is to remove that vital entry to dummy's long Diamond suit.

(4) The Spade Jack. West has five tricks in sight, enough to set declarer. Don't waste time knocking out dummy's Heart entry.

(5) A low Diamond. The opponents have seven Diamonds. If they are divided 4-3 the contract is in the bag. If they are 5-2, declarer has to find the Heart Ace with South to land his contract.

(6) If South needs five tricks, he cannot afford to duck. However, if he needs only four he can make the safety play of ducking once. This allows for a 4-1 split of the outstanding Clubs.

IV. Point Count

(1) Pass, 13 points – 1 for no Aces.

(2) 1 Spade, bid the longest suit first. Any five-card suit is biddable. $14 + 2 = 16$ points.

(3) 1 Spade. Your hand is too good to preempt, and the points aren't concentrated in the trump suit. $11 + 3 = 14$.

(4) 1 Club. You have No Trump distribution but only 15 points, not sufficient to open a No Trump.

(5) Re-evaluated, your hand is worth 15. Pass. The most partner possibly can have is 10. No game is in sight.

(6) Re-evaluating the baby Spades, your hand is worth 18. Invite game by bidding 3 Spades.

(7) Re-evaluating your Spade length sends you to 22. Bid 4 Spades. When the opener sees game he goes.

(8) Pass. You've bid your hand to the hilt.

(9) Invite game with 3 Spades. Your hand is worth 12 points.

(10) Bid 4 Spades. Don't muddy the waters by showing the Club fit. Your hand values at 13 points and the partnership has nine cards in the Spade suit. Contract for the major suit game. Tip, don't value your hand as if it were dummy. You're declarer now.

(11) You hold $9 + 4 = 13$. Jump to 3 Hearts. Do not confuse the bidding with a Spade call. A trump suit has been discovered; make the glorious announcement.

(12) Pass. $3 + 2 = 5$. The way to tell partner you don't have 6 points is to pass.

(13) Bid 1 Spade. You have 17 high-card points. Keep the bidding at a low level while looking for a trump suit. After you find one, you may wish to make a slam try. Don't

give too much value to your Heart singleton until you find what you are going to use for trumps.

(14) 4 + 4 = 8. Bid 2 Hearts.

V. Rebid By Opener

1. 2 Spades to show a minimum.
   3 Spades to show 16-18 and invite game.
   4 Spades. You see game, bid it.

2. 2 Clubs.
   2 Clubs, a new suit shows a minimum or medium hand.

   Jump to 3 Clubs, forcing, showing 19-21 points.

3. 1 No Trump, minimum hand, even distribution.
   Bid 2 NT to invite game.
   Jump to 3 No Trump showing 20 or 21 points.

4. 2 Hearts, rebidding your major shows a six-card suit, minimum hand.

   Jump to 3 Hearts. A jump in your original suit shows 16-18, and a strong suit.

   Jump to 4 Hearts, or make-up a suit for a jump shift (Clubs) to show your 20 points and force partner to speak again.

5. Pass. You have a minimum and even distribution. Don't worry about Clubs.

   Bid 2 No Trump to invite game.
   3 No Trump, jump one level with 19.

6. 3 Clubs, a single raise of partner's suit shows a minimum.

   4 Clubs, a jump in partner's suit shows 16-18.

   4 No Trump, looking for a slam. Even if partner answers 5 Clubs, showing no Aces, bid 6 Clubs. There is a play for 12 tricks.

7. 2 Hearts, the only bid available that says "I have a minimum opener." You're promising six cards in your suit and you don't have them. You have to tell partner a story about your distribution or your point-count. Don't lie about your point-count.

2 Spades, a reverse, forcing the bidding to the three level. Shows a big hand of 17 points or more.

Just bid 2 Spades. You have the points for a jump-shift, but you don't know yet where you're going to play the hand. The bidding isn't going to die. Partner's bid of a new suit at the 2-level (showing 10 points or more) promises another bid.

8. Pass. There's no hope for game.

Bid 3 Hearts to invite game with your 14 + 3 = 17.

Jump to 4 Hearts.

VI. Responder Rebids

1. (a) Partner is bidding like a man with five Spades (or six).

(b) He has five Hearts; he would not rebid a four-card suit. He said he has no desire to play No Trump.

(c) He has a minimum hand of 13-15 because he did not jump the bidding when he rebid Hearts.

(d) No.

(e) Partner's hand may be ♠ AQxxx ♡AQxxx ◊ x ♣ xx. The crucial cards missing are the Club Ace, the Spade King, and the Heart King. If any one is well placed, partner has a chance. Bid 4 Hearts.

2. (a) He probably has four Clubs but could hold five (since he didn't like your No Trump bid, he sounds like he has a Diamond singleton or an empty doubleton.)

(b) He has specifically four Spades.

(c) He has only three Hearts. If he had four, he would have raised Hearts immediately, not bid Spades.

(d) He has a medium hand, 16-18, which he revealed when he made the jump raise in Hearts.

(e) 4 Hearts. Partner's hand is something like SA10xx, HKQx, Dx, CAK10xx.

3. (a) Rebidding his major showed six cards or a strong five.

(b) A minimum hand, 13 to 15 points.

(c) Pass.

4. (a) Five hearts, though it could be more.

(b) Four Spades for the immediate raise.

(c) He has a maximum opener with 19-21 points.

(d) 4 NT, running up the slam flag.

5. (a) He has five; with six, he would prefer to rebid Spades.

(b) He has two Hearts. Since you showed five when you bid them at the 2-level, he would have raised with three. He wouldn't rebid NT without even distribution. He would have a second suit to bid if he had only one Heart.

(c) He has three of each; his distribution is 5-2-3-3.

(d) Minimum hand, 13-15. Probably on the top side, 15.

(e) 3 NT. Don't worry about Diamonds. Partner has some face cards.

VII. Opening Leads

Against No Trump

1. The Spade 3, fourth-best of the longest and strongest suit.

2. The Heart Jack, top of an interior sequence. Awkward if declarer holds Ace-Queen, but still the best chance to set the contract.

3. Heart 4, prefer a major to a minor.

4. The Spade Jack, less risky than Clubs, and with better prospects. If declarer holds the King-Queen and wins one, partner may get in and lead through the other honor.

5. The Heart Queen is safe and might develop two tricks. With one more Spade prefer Spades.

6. The Spade 7, in case partner only has two, you're leaving one in his hand so he can return your suit.

7. The Heart Queen. Save the Spades for entries to establish Hearts.

Against Clubs

1. Diamond Queen, top of a sequence.

2. Spade 2, low from a single honor.

3. Spade Ace, trying for a ruff.

4. The Spade Ace. With lots of trumps lead your longest suit.

5. Heart Queen, top of a sequence.

6. Spade King and watch partner's card. If he has a doubleton, he can trump the third round.

7. Spade King. Get your sure tricks quickly in a suit contract.

8. The Spade 10, an unbid major. With no entries try to guess partner's suit.

8. You have lots of trumps so lead your longest suit, it's a guess, Spades or Diamonds, probably Spade 10.

9. The Diamond King, top of a doubleton of partner's suit.

10. The Spade 9. Win the first round of trumps and put partner in with a Diamond to give you a Spade ruff. If partner happens to have the Spade Ace and the Diamond Ace, you can get two ruffs and set this hand before declarer even gets on lead.

11. Diamond 3, your partner's suit, and your fourth-best. A good lead for two reasons. First, your partner bid it. Second, you have lots of trumps. You hope declarer is going to have to ruff and shorten his trump holding. Do not lead the singleton; if you trumped Spades it would shorten you in trumps.

12. It sounds like a cross-ruff, so the best defense is a trump lead. Play the Heart 9. When you regain the lead, press on with another Heart. Cut down on Spade ruffs in dummy.

13. Spade 5, your fourth-best. Partner's double asked you to lead your suit. He has a card that will help you, probably the Queen. Without the lead-indicating double prefer the Heart King, top of an imperfect sequence, and less likely to present declarer with a trick.

VIII. Defensive Overcalls

(1) Say 2 Hearts. You have an opening hand and a good suit.

(2) Pass. You're not strong enough in points or suit to come in at the 2-level.

(3) Pass. Wouldn't you rather play Spades than anything else? That's where you are!

(4) Jump to 3 Hearts, a preemptive bid. You'll probably bring in six tricks in your hand alone, overbidding three tricks not vulnerable.

(5) With a two-suited hand, start overcalling. Bid 2 Diamonds.

(6) You have an opening hand, but it is wise to pass; you have too much in the opener's suit.

(7) Raise to 2 Hearts. You couldn't bid with less, but you don't promise more.

(8) Pass. Let the opponents play it; save competitive bidding for hands where you and partner have a fit.

(9) Bid 2 Hearts. You're assured of an eight-card trump suit. Don't try Spades; you don't need two trump suits.

(10) Bid 2 Spades. Your suit is strong enough to bid at the 2-level and you can't raise Hearts.

(11) Bid 2 No Trump. With 11 points you want to compete.

(12) Pass. Don't bid No Trump; you haven't a balanced hand.

(13) Bid 4 Hearts. Let the opponents decide what to do at that high level. If partner goes down, as he might, the opponents missed something.

(14) Bid 2 NT. You want to take some action with 12 points. There might still be a game for you.

IX. Other Defensive Bids

(1) Cue bid 3 Clubs. You're prepared to carry on to game in either major. Let partner choose his favorite.

(2) Bid 4 Hearts, though your suit isn't robust. You have an excellent fit with partner, who obviously has a Club singleton or a void.

(3) Bid 2 No Trump to describe your balanced hand and 10 points. Don't worry about Hearts; partner has something there. He promised help in the majors.

(4) Bid 2 Diamonds. It's time again for prayers.

(5) Raise to 2 Spades. As a dummy, your hand values at 17, with a plus for your body cards. Game is still possible.

(6) Rebid 1 No Trump to show a balanced hand that was too strong to overcall a No Trump, 19-20 points.

(7) Pass. You have the barest of bare take-out doubles. There's no hope for a game if partner can't jump.

(8) Make a jump-raise to 3 Spades to show the trump fit and 19-21 points. This is a strong game invitation; partner needs very little to accept.

(9) Bid 2 Spades. You have a powerful hand and a reasonable chance for game in any other suit.

(10) Double. If partner responds 2 Clubs, bid 2 Hearts. If he responds 2 Hearts or 2 Diamonds, give a single raise.

(11) Overcall 2 Hearts although your suit is weak. If you get into trouble you have a place to run, Clubs.

(12) Bid 2 Diamonds, a cue-bid. You have a game-going hand, but it is better not to plough right into 4 Spades or 4 Hearts, guessing which would be better. The cue-bid asks partner to choose the suit. You plan to bid game in whichever he chooses.

X Signaling

(1) (a) The Diamond Ace, and then the Jack. East's 9 looks like the beginning of a high-low signal showing a doubleton. He'll trump the third round. Continuing with the Jack is a Suit Preference Signal asking for a Heart return. Setting this contract looks like a sure thing!

(b) If partner has a doubleton, so does declarer who will be able to over-ruff. Your chances of sinking the contract are dim unless partner's Diamond 9 is a singleton.

(2) The Heart 9, an encouraging card, beginning the high-low signal. Prefer it to the 7 because it speaks louder.

(3) The Ace of Spades. Partner is asking for a switch, but West is vetoing the recommendation. West has declarer set in his own hand. He continues Spades, gives declarer his Queen, and when he gets in with the vital Diamond Ace, he'll have enough tricks to sink this contract.

(4) (a) The Heart 3. You urgently desire a Club play. Concentrate on that message.

(b) The Diamond deuce to say you don't like Diamonds either. The count signal isn't important here.

(c) The deuce of Spades. Now you've told your story by inference; you adore Clubs but you can't afford to discard one. Declarer might hold four to the Club 9.

(5) The Spade 2 and next the Club 2 to send word he desires a Heart. East cannot afford to discard a Heart. He needs every one he has to set the contract.

(6) The Diamond 5, the smallest he has, a Suit Preference Signal telling partner he has an entry in Clubs.

(7) The Club Jack urgently signaling for a Club lead. East can afford a high one because his four Clubs plus partner's entry is enough to set declarer. With only four Clubs he'd have to play the Heart 2, signaling by inference.

(8) East should play his lowest, the 3, to discourage a continuation. Declarer falsecards with the 8, hoping to hoodwink West into continuing the suit because it's the only way South can win a trick with the Queen.

(9) Partner's trump echo shows he holds a third trump and wants to ruff. Play the Heart King, and then another Heart for partner to ruff. Choose the Heart 10, which asks for a Diamond return.